THE CHILD CARE WORKER
Concepts, Tasks and Relationships

The Child Care Worker

Concepts, Tasks and Relationships

by

JACK ADLER, Ed.D., A.C.S.W.

Coordinator of Staff Development
Jewish Child Care Association of New York

BRUNNER/MAZEL, *Publishers*   •   New York

Library of Congress Cataloging in Publication Data
Adler, Jack, 1916-
    The child care worker.

    Bibliography: p. 187
    Includes index.
    1.   Children—Institutional care.   I.   Title.
HV873.A34   362.7   76-15570
ISBN 0-87630-125-1

Published by

BRUNNER/MAZEL, INC.
19 Union Square West, New York, N. Y. 10003

MANUFACTURED IN THE UNITED STATES OF AMERICA

To my wife Myril and our children, David and Sharon.
To all children in residential care and their
child care workers.

Preface

The preparation of this book has been motivated by the desire to share with child care workers everywhere the content of an introductory seminar given by the author in various group programs of the Jewish Child Care Association.* The basic content of the seminar was found to be adaptable to the diverse settings in which it was given. Among these were four residential treatment centers—Childville, for severely disturbed young children, Edenwald School, for multi-handicapped, mildly retarded children, Pleasantville Cottage School, for emotionally disturbed boys and girls, and Youth Residence Center, a community-based center for young adults —as well as the Diagnostic Center at Pleasantville, and Vernondale, a group apartment unit for physically handicapped children.

* The Jewish Child Care Association serves about 1,300 neglected, dependent and emotionally disturbed children in a variety of foster care placements including foster homes, group homes, group residences and residential treatment centers. Also a diagnostic center serves about 200 children annually. Its day care program includes a day care center for preschool children and a day treatment program for emotionally disturbed children. A central intake service, the Joint Planning Service, is jointly operated by the Jewish Child Care Association and the Jewish Board of Guardians. There is also a central aftercare service.

The issues and concepts introduced by the seminar leader were supplemented by examples from daily practice presented by participating child care workers. Discussion was not limited to clarifying basic issues and concepts, but extended to problem solving. Critical incidents and specific management problems from daily practice were analyzed. In a number of the seminars, administrative and child care supervisory staff attended as participant observers. When general topics such as administration, diagnosis, education, psychiatry, psychological testing, recreation, and social work were discussed, representatives from these disciplines were invited discussants.

This book is designed for child care workers in all types of residential settings, including general institutions which care for the so-called "normal but dependent and neglected" children (Kadushin, 1967, p. 517)—the largest group of children in institutional foster care. The term "normal" is neither appropriate nor adequate as a description of dependent and neglected children. All of them have experienced varying degrees of emotional trauma as a consequence of their family life situations, including conditions of poverty, family disorganization and parental disturbance. These factors, culminating in separation from their families, have generated anxieties, anger, a sense of inadequacy and distrust of others. These children require as much sensitivity and understanding as children classified as "emotionally disturbed" in residential treatment centers.

In orienting new child care workers, this book should be supplemented by written material which explains the routines and regulations and treatment philosophy specific to a particular residential program. It is also advisable to include historical material about the institution and the parent agency.

Part III—*Tasks*—includes a series of guiding questions on observing individual children and groups, plus self-observation questions for the child care workers. These may facilitate evaluation and understanding of a child's personality assets, as well as of his behavioral difficulties and lags in development. Group observation familiarizes the worker with his group's interactions—destructive tendencies as well as potential strengths. The self-awareness questions provide a reflective framework for the worker. As a unit, they illuminate the complexity of the child care worker's role in living with children of stress.

The difficulties faced by child care workers can be very taxing. Consequently, a statement of concepts and standards of child care practice should represent guidelines for goals to be achieved. The process of realization, through acquisition of knowledge and skills, integration of experience, development of self-awareness, and modification of attitudes, takes time. It is hoped that this book will serve to facilitate this process of becoming.

REFERENCE

KADUSHIN, ALFRED, *Child Welfare Services*. New York, Macmillan, 1967.

Acknowledgments

I wish to thank my colleagues at Childville, Diagnostic Center, Edenwald School, Pleasantville Cottage School, Youth Residence Center and Vernondale, who participated in the seminars given at the Jewish Child Care Association of New York. They shared views and contributed insights and examples cited. Some of the formulations and examples date back to the years of association with the Hawthorne Cedar Knolls School of the Jewish Board of Guardians, where I had direct child care experience with children of stress and supervised child care workers in addition to individual and group therapy responsibility. I am particularly grateful to my recently deceased colleague and friend, Irwin Berman, fondly known to all as Bud, for sharing his extensive knowledge and brilliant insights about emotionally disturbed children and residential treatment.

I am grateful to the following publications for the use of material which, in modified form, previously appeared in my published articles: *Child Welfare* for "General Concepts in Residential Treatment of Disturbed Children," Vol. 47, No. 9, November, 1968; "The Delinquent-Oriented Adolescent in Residential Placement," Vol. 48, No. 3, 1969; and "Interpersonal Relationships in Residential Treatment Centers for Disturbed Children," Vol. 1, No. 4, April, 1971; *Journal of Jewish Communal Services* for "Separation: A Crucial Issue in Foster Care," Vol. XLVI, No. 4, Summer, 1970; and *Child Care Quarterly* for "The Child Care Counselor as Target of Transferred Behavior," July, 1973.

I warmly thank Dr. Sol Nichtern for encouraging me in writing this book and for use of quotes and facts on child development from his book, *Helping the Retarded Child* (New York, Grosset and Dunlap, 1974). Thanks are also due to Herman Stern, Director of Edenwald School, for permission to quote from the Edenwald School *Manual of Policies and Procedures,* to Peter Parnell and Rhoda Cobin for the quotes from *Health Care Procedures,* and to the American Psychiatric Association for the material in the Appendix which is based on the *Diagnostic and Statistical Manual of Mental Disorders,* 2nd Edition, Washington, D.C., 1968.

I offer sincere thanks to Estelle Plung and Beatrice Sherman for their work in editing the book, and to Adriane Grunberg for typing the manuscript.

Above all, I am indebted to all of the children and their child care workers, who were my most challenging teachers of residential treatment.

Contents

CONTENTS

Introduction

Children are a wonderment. They deify and involve us with ultimate creativity—the initiation of life (conception), the production of life (child bearing) and the molding of life (child rearing). They reinforce our awareness of the energy and the potential of all living things.

Sol Nichtern

This poetic statement represents the gift of childhood to the adult world. It is within each child to offer it, but regretfully not within every adult's capacity to cherish it, to actualize its potential rewards in the enriching experience of parenthood. Even the child born with a defect which will limit his physical, mental and emotional development bears this potential gift for the parents who have the strength, maturity and love to cope with the additional care which will be required in rearing a handicapped child (Nichtern, 1974, p. 9).

There are parents who cannot provide their children with minimal nurturing needs of childhood, such as a physical environment which is safe, comfortable and clean to protect their safety and health, adequate food, shelter, and clothing on a predictable basis, and emotional ties with family members in which children experience themselves as valued, important, and belonging. Children also require opportunities for other supportive relationships outside of the home, activities and interests which contribute to their social and intellectual development. They need parental guidance and involvement in education, cultural identification and acquisition of moral and ethical values (Sister Mary Paul, 1975, p. 5).

When parents are unable to provide for their children's developmental needs it is due to a variety of social and personal factors. It may result from pressures stemming from chronic conditions of poverty and social discrimination. Children growing up in families locked into the "cycle of poverty"—poverty that extends from generation to generation—are truly disadvantaged in all phases of their development by socioeconomic forces beyond the control of their parents. They do not have the opportunity to develop to their fullest potential. Their nurture and socialization are affected by family patterns which are a consequence of long-term deprivations and lack of opportunity. Many of these families become "multi-problem" families with a high degree of dependency, instability and deficiency from community and social norms. Their children are most likely to be neglected or to get into difficulties at home, at school, and in the neighborhood (Billingsley, 1968, p. 144).

Parents may also be incapacitated by physical and emotional illness. And there are parents who are unwilling to assume parental responsibility. In a recent study of foster care in New York City, 30.6% of the children were in placement because of "parental unwillingness to care for child, including desertion" (Bernstein et al., 1975, p. 11).

Family disorganization, the end product of multiple family problems, which accounts for placement of the vast majority of children, could be markedly reduced by supportive services to families under social and personal stress. For example, it is estimated that over 4,000 children currently in foster care or awaiting placement in New York City (where social and health services are probably more developed and extensive than in most of our urban centers) could be maintained in their own homes if such services were available. This would include homemaker, housing assistance, casework and child guidance, day care and day treatment, recreation, special education and drug rehabilitation services. The benefit to the community would be twofold—conservation of family intactness and economic savings. The cost of the preventive services is estimated to be a fraction of the current cost of foster care (Bernstein et al., 1975, p. 97). With appropriate community services, many parents could also care for a physically, intellectually or emotionally handicapped child in ther homes, avoiding hospital or institutional placement.

There are, however, children who require specialized services which under the best of circumstances could not be provided within a family setting. Some require temporary, others long-term care, and a residue will need lifelong institutional supports.

Based on statistics of the late 1960s, there were about 195,000 children in the United States served in 2,300 institutions, employing about 29,000 full-time child care workers (American Association for Children's Residential Centers, 1972, p. 100). In New York City alone, as of December, 1974, approximately 29,000 children were in foster care. Of these, 7,800 were in group residences and institutional settings, including residential treatment centers. The projection for the future envisions increased numbers of children requiring care in group homes and residential treatment (Bernstein, 1975, p. 64).

During the past decade, children referred for placement

have been more severely disturbed than in previous years. This may be a consequence of changing conditions in our society. Greater family mobility, the ever increasing number of working mothers, strains of urban life in deteriorating neighborhoods and higher divorce rates have contributed to more extensive family instability and disorganization. Advances in medical sciences and broader distribution of medical and social services have resulted in higher survival rates among seriously handicapped children. Changing hospital policies have drastically curtailed long-term hospitalization of emotionally disturbed and mentally ill children. Many more of these children are being referred to child welfare agencies for residential treatment.

Increased numbers of effectively trained child care workers are needed to serve these severely disturbed children. The universal recognition that the child care worker is a very significant person for children in placement has to be complemented by more extensive provisions for education and in-service training. "Basic training is essential to achieve professional identification, increased resources of staff, transferability of knowledge and skill from one institution to another" (American Association for Children's Residential Centers, 1972, p. 100).

Advances have been made in developing formal educational programs for child care workers in two-year programs in community colleges and undergraduate college programs. These include didactic courses, as well as supervised field instruction. There is also a beginning trend in furthering education of child care workers on the basis of the Canadian psycho-educateur model which is an intensive and comprehensive four-year educational program to prepare a child care worker to function as the chief professional person in a child's residential treatment (Guindon, 1973, pp. 27-32).

Currently, the majority of child care workers continue to

be utilized in a caretaking or substitute parent role. In residential treatment centers, their role and function are affected by the dominant treatment philosophy of the institution. This may be the psychoanalytic model which strives for changes in personality within the child, the educative approach which utilizes behavior modification techniques and learning reinforcement to achieve changes in specific maladaptive behavior, the existential model which relies on group process and student government, the medical model concentrating on prescription of medication and psychotherapy, the family model replicating the child's family experience (American Association for Children's Residential Centers, 1972, p. 103), or a combination of any of the above.

The varied treatment approaches may affect the child care worker's "method" of relating to the children but not the "substance" of his* tasks. These derive from care of children during the twenty-four hour spectrum of daily living. They include supervision of daily activities from waking to bedtime, relationships with individual children and groups, recording observations and consultation with other staff. The knowledge and skills associated with these responsibilities have to be made available to every child care worker through in-service training, seminars and supervision. A fundamental understanding of "normal" child development, as well as of the deviations which bring children into residential treatment, is also essential.

This book addresses itself directly to child care workers regarding the fundamental issues involved in living with and caring for children of stress. We believe that with minor adaptations it can be utilized in orienting child care workers to practice in institutions of diverse theoretical and treatment approaches.

---

* The use of the masculine gender "he" incorporates the feminine "she" in accordance with grammatical usage. It is not due to lack of respect or admiration for women child care workers. The same applies to references to a child as "he."

The content reflects the author's orientation towards psychodynamic psychology and social system theories, which view the child as the product of biological endowment and environmental nurture. The influence of the unconscious motivation on expressed behavior is also considered pertinent. From the beginning of his life the child is affected by social interactions and the emotions and behavior they generate among members of his immediate family. His environment is also influenced by outside social forces.

The focus and concern of child care should be the child, representing a "whole" being, rather than control of symptomatic behavior which causes maladaptive reactions in the living situation. The reeducative or "treatment" process requires that its methods adapt to a child's needs rather than to a particular treatment philosophy and technology. The child must be understood as an individual and as a member of a peer group, functioning in a variety of situations and relationships. The "helping" adults, representing diverse disciplines, are dedicated to his growth and development and his return to his family and community as a more mature being.

REFERENCES

American Association for Children's Residential Centers, *From Chaos to Order—A Collective View of the Residential Treatment of Children.* New York, Child Welfare League of America, 1972.

BERNSTEIN, BLANCHE ET AL., *A Preliminary Report—Foster Care Needs and Alternatives to Placement—A Projection for 1975-85.* N.Y. State Department of Social Welfare, June, 1975.

BILLINGSLEY, ANDREW, *Black Families in White America.* Englewood Cliffs, N.J., Prentice-Hall, 1968.

GUINDON, JEANNINE, "The Psychoeducateur Training Program." *International Journal of Mental Health,* Vol. 2, No. 1, pp. 27-32, 1973.

NICHTERN, SOL, *Helping the Retarded Child.* New York, Grosset & Dunlap, 1974.

PAUL, SISTER MARY, *Criteria for Foster Placement and Alternatives to Foster Care.* N.Y. State Board of Social Welfare, May, 1975.

THE CHILD CARE WORKER
Concepts, Tasks and Relationships

1. Concepts

A residential treatment center is a therapeutic community, and as such it is a complex organism. As a community it has a culture of its own, but it is not isolated from influences of the greater community that impinge on it. The interpersonal interactions it generates represent its dynamism, and its treatment philosophy its essence (Adler, 1968).

COMPONENTS OF RESIDENTIAL TREATMENT

The basic components of residential treatment generally include the following:

1. *A therapeutic environment* which provides the children with corrective or restitutive experiences through a framework of planned and structured activities, education, socialization and identifications with positive adult models. It involves the disciplines of child care, education, religion, recreation, and medical services.

2. *Casework and Psychotherapeutic Services* include
psychosocial assessment of each child (and his family) and individual and/or group therapy sessions. The
scope of individual and group psychotherapeutic techniques made available to a child depends on his developmental level, degree of disturbance and motivation. These help him evaluate his reactions to the
controlled environment in which he lives, his feelings
about himself and others, his reality functioning, his
perceptions and distortions of past and current experiences. If he has a family, they become part of
the overall rehabilitation effort. The differential use
of these services is important since it is not at all
certain that all children in placement are in need of or
can profit from intensive psychotherapy. The disciplines involved include psychiatry, psychology and
social work.

3. *Integration* or synthesis of the environmental and
psychotherapeutic components is essential and is
achieved by ongoing communication among the various disciplines involved with the child. This implies
joint planning, evaluation and implementation of
treatment objectives.

CONCEPTS OF RESIDENTIAL TREATMENT

The following concepts and principles of residential treatment of disturbed children are based on psychological and
sociological theories, including role theory and group dynamics, as well as pragmatic experience in residential treatment.

Residential Treatment as Planned and Controlled Living

The child who comes to an institution has generally experienced failure in many aspects of his life. He needs to establish order in his disorganized mode of living. To achieve harmony from disorder he must first experience ordered and planned living. The "structure" of the institution represents a fundamental therapeutic component of residential treatment. It should provide a life rhythm of routines and expectations. This tends to diminish conflict because there are fewer individual choices about routines of daily living. It represents concreteness, rather than vagueness, certainty rather than confusion, and simplification instead of complexity.

Another aspect of structure is protection against destructive impulse expression. Just as society prescribes rules of conduct and laws for the protection of all, so does the residential center provide its children with external controls against destructive impulses which may be inadequately controlled from within. Destructive acts against oneself, against others and against property are dealt with quickly and effectively. If this is not done, adult inaction may be interpreted as indirect approval of destructive behavior. This may convey adult weakness and indecision to children who require adult firmness and strength.

Because structure is imposed and restrictive, it tends to evoke anxieties and frustration. It should therefore be clearly interpreted and consistently administered. Children who have conflict about it should have an opportunity to discuss it. Adolescents, in particular, are more apt to accept it and conform to its requirements when they are convinced that "rules" are not arbitrarily set by each individual adult but are responsibly planned (Mayer, 1972, p. 487). When structure is equivalent to controls, without considering therapeutic needs of children, when it has no flexibility to adapt to an individual's developing capacity for greater responsibility, it becomes rigid stultifying, and losing its therapeutic value. When overemphasis on controls is motivated by the need of an institution's staff to maintain order and to avoid trouble, it may not be constructive as a method of rehabilitation. An inflexible institutional program dominated by rigid rules and sanctions may suffice for containment purposes. It may achieve superficial conformity and adaptation to the institution's standards because of fear of adult retaliation, but it will not generally promote inner change. The street-wise youngster may pay lip service to the adult-dominated social structure. He is capable of manipulating adults for his benefit. His adjustment may seem impressive but it is superficial. He adapts but he does not change. If he has leadership capabilities, he may in fact rule a cottage group in accordance with an accustomed delinquent code and hinder others from benefiting from a rehabilitation program (Polsky, 1962). Structure should not be fixed or rigid. It should have a built-in flexibility for the youngster who has demonstrated a capacity for greater responsibility and independence.

It is not sufficient for staff to be familiar with the structure of the institution and to carry out its requirements with efficiency. Acceptance and understanding of its therapeutic purposes are essential, and staff must have the capacity to convey these feelings with conviction and firmness but without hostility or defensiveness. If a worker is dissatisfied with a prescribed rule or routine and therefore finds it difficult to enforce, he should discuss it with his supervisor. Change or deviations from established practice cannot be left to the discretion of an individual. They require prior discussion among staff and, wherever feasible, with the children as well.

Authority

Every individual relates to authority figures. Child development requires authority as well as love. It is an essential aspect of parenthood and parental guidance. Children's ambivalence about adult authority is an age-old phenomenon, and recent years have witnessed increasing parental ambivalence about exercising authority. Mayer (1972, p. 484) states:

> What has made the handling of adolescents complicated in our time is not that today's adolescents are so much more opposed than in the past to the use of authority (Socrates complained about the unruliness and rebelliousness of the young), but rather that adults have become so much more uncertain and guilt-stricken about using authority.

To be constructive, the adult acting in an authority role cannot be authoritarian, meaning despotic, rigid, unsympathetic or cruel. If he is, he will be feared but not respected. Neither can he be corruptible or subject to manipulation. If he is, he may be subject to seduction by the shrewd, exploited by the strong, considered hypocritical by all and respected by no one.

The child care worker by his very role and function represents authority. He can expect to evoke ambivalent feelings among all of the children and overt resistance by some. This is particularly pertinent in relation to the delinquent-oriented adolescent who views adults, with the exception of his delinquent associates, as tyrannical authority figures. He tends to express his hostility by defiance and destructive acts. In residential treatment, such a youngster may be helped to modify his distorted attitudes by making available to him benign, firm and uncorruptible adults with whom he may establish a significant relationship. There must also exist an atmosphere of respect for authority. If a child care worker conveys to children the impression that he is conflicted about authority, or feels guilty about expressing it, he cannot be an effective authority figure. He may, in fact, fortify conflicting feelings toward authority.

Emphasis on Health

No matter how disturbed a child may be, he has vestiges of health within him which have to be identified and nurtured. Since children's recuperative powers are strong, they have a chance to develop when they are transferred from pathogenic environmental conditions.

The assessment of a child's strengths is most important. It complements diagnostic understanding of his disturbance or handicap by identifying potential sources of health. This is useful in planning a program of activities for him which match assigned tasks with his capabilities. It will enhance the likelihood of success in mastering physical, intellectual and social skills. Mastery opportunities built into the residential program include learning and work responsibilities in the cottage, at school and in leisure time activities. Geared to high but flexible standards of expectations they help increase a sense of adequacy and self-confidence. Adults convey to the children the feeling that they believe in their capacities and potentials. This involves an understanding of a child's strengths, a readiness to help him with problems of mastery, and a flexible, increasing scale of tasks and expectations.

Group Living and Individualization

The child in a residential setting lives in groups and is constantly subjected to the demands and pressures of group living. Understanding the meaning of group living for the individual child, as well as his own impact on the group, is important. For example, a child with pathological needs tends to express them behaviorally in relationships with his peers and staff. The delinquent-oriented youngster will strive to perpetuate his former gang culture within his cottage group by seeking out others to join him in reenacting aggressive and destructive behavior.

Child care workers are often troubled by what seem to them to be clinician's pressures for "individualizing" without due regard for the realities of managing a group of troubled and troublesome children. It is not uncommon to hear a worker say, "I understand that Johnny requires more of my attention but to give it I have to neglect someone else. . . ." Or, "If I give Mary this additional privilege, the other girls will accuse me of favoring her and of not liking them."

This is an understandable dilemma. However, there does not need to be a dichotomy between individual needs and the group. The uniqueness of the individual must not be neglected for the benefit of group control. Although group living should be designed to provide optimum growth possibilities for each child, one cannot expect child care workers (or teachers) to disregard group needs to meet an individual child's excessive needs for physical care, attention or special treatment. When such a child is introduced to a group, there needs to be supervisory understanding that he will require special attention and administrative responsibility to insure that there will be adequate staff coverage to meet his needs so that the regular staff will not be overburdened nor the other children neglected.

It is important for staff, as well as children, to accept the principle that individualization is a prime focus of residential treatment. The group, as a dynamic balance of interacting individuals, serves as a medium which enhances individual development. This implies educating everyone, especially the children, to understand the concept of individuality—that each one is cherished as unique, and every child's needs will be respected as much as it is possible. If a child needs something "extra" or some special attention, it does not mean that it is given at the expense of the others, that the motive is to be unfair, discriminating or "undemocratic." When a child accepts this interpretation and can act upon it, he has matured from self-interest to respecting others' needs, from distrust to trustfulness, and demonstrates a readiness and capacity to share a significant adult with another child without feeling rejected.

There are innumerable examples in residential treatment to illustrate individualization. One deals quite differently with two children who may commit the same type of offense against institutional structure. For example, when a psychotic child is "out of place" from his school program, one takes into consideration that he is a disoriented child who frequently forgets where he is and what he is supposed to be doing. Such a child is helped to get back to his class. When a sociopathic type youngster tries to manipulate himself out of the classroom situation in order to do as he pleases, he is treated with firmness and may be punished if the offense is repeated. One individualizes in many other respects—the number of times a child is seen in individual therapy, the type of school program to which he is assigned, his cottage group placement, his recreation group assignments, etc.

However, overall institutional structure sets the outer boundaries beyond which individualization is not possible. If these limits are overextended, the total program might be threatened by disorganization. For example, delinquent acting out cannot be condoned. Consistent and uniform attitudes must be conveyed against runaways, against destruction of property and against physical assault. Neither should the structure of daily routines, such as getting up on time, cleanliness of the cottage, mealtimes, bedtime, etc. be discarded because of individualization.

Identification

Identification plays a major role in human development. Unlike imitation, it operates unconsciously. The individual strives to pattern himself after a person or persons significant in his life by incorporating his attributes, beliefs and values.

Many of the children in residential settings have not experienced wholesome relationships with adults within their own families. Consequently, their identifications may be confused, diffused or faulty through association with asocial or antisocial models. In residential treatment, efforts are made to help them overcome their reservations and resistances to form significant relationships with adults. This may pave the way toward positive identifications.

Esthetic values, pertaining to a sense of the beautiful, are important in achieving constructive and mature identifications. A person's physical environment affects his state of well-being, and is a determinant in the development of his creative potential. It is the institution's responsibility to make available to children a living situation and activities which evoke and encourage creative expression. This may be done by making the children's physical surroundings attractive, and by actively sensitizing staff and children to esthetic values in relation to cleanliness, appearance and tidiness in cottage and classroom. The key factor seems to be the attitudes of the adults around them. If they set sound standards, and are actively involved in attaining and maintaining them, they will convey to the children that they care for them and that they, the children, are worth caring for. On the other hand, the children tend to respond with apathy or even destructiveness to drab and shabby physical surroundings. Maintenance of standards may be an ongoing struggle for many workers because of children's inability or unwillingness to comply, but standards should not be compromised.

Ethics, which may be viewed as the quality that integrates human beings into a society, are also important in achieving mature identifications. Ethical values are a gauge of a civilization's spiritual and social achievement, as well as man's counterforce against the pressures of destructive inner impulses. Laws representing ethical and moral values have been in existence throughout man's recorded history. Children are taught to respect laws, but they inevitably become aware of the existence of a gap between the ethical values they are taught and expected to follow and their violation by adults in daily life transactions. When this occurs they may begin to view adult teaching with skepticism. It is unlikely that they will incorporate adult values unless they are convinced that adults adhere to them.

Cultural, ethnic and religious factors are important aspects of a person's sense of identity. The cottage group, consisting of children representing a diversity of cultural, ethnic and religious backgrounds, can serve and enhance such identifications and correct prejudices. An essential requirement for its realization is staff attitudes. If a child care worker has confused identifications and manifests prejudiced attitudes, he will convey this to the children. This may result not only in confusion on the children's part, but, at its worst, an enhancement of prejudice. Awareness of one's own feelings and attitudes is helpful. A genuine expression of tolerance and respect for differences by the adults will be felt by the children. This in time may help them modify their own prejudiced attitudes and behavior toward others who are different.

Community

A residential facility is generally a self-contained entity for the children and a meaningful community for its resident staff. A sense of being an integral part of this community is important for all. Each staff member needs to feel a sense of security of his status and recognition for his contribution. This is especially important in the case of child care personnel who reside in the institution. If conditions are pleasant, their feelings of satisfaction will outweigh the tensions inherent in the strains of daily living with groups of disturbed children.

Integration

In a residential treatment setting no one can be fully effective working in isolation. Positive results can be achieved only through collective effort and cooperation. Such "integration" goes beyond sharing of information among the various disciplines. It involves joint planning and evaluation of a child's treatment plan, a capacity to work together, respect for contributions made by each member of the residential "team," a common conception of the work, and an understanding of the complementarity of each other's roles and tasks. The clinical and environmental programs must function as a unified therapeutic effort through participation of all of the disciplines in planning for each child, implementing individual and group treatment goals and evaluating the overall program of the institution.

Disunity and role confusion among staff are not helpful to children, especially to those who have witnessed parental disharmony. One area of confusion in relation to role may arise when there is no common base of reference about basic terminology. For example, the term "treatment" in the very designation of the institution as a residential treatment center may mean different things to teachers, social workers, child care workers or psychiatrists. If it is viewed in its specific circumscribed meaning, connoting individual psychotherapy, rather than the broad growth-inducing and rehabilitation services the institution makes available for the children, it is a distortion of the essence of residential treatment. "Treatment" signifies the total encompassing atmosphere and practice in a residential treatment center and includes all of the aspects of the therapeutic milieu and clinical services.

All personnel working with children in a residential treatment center must function therapeutically. This means that each one addresses himself to the individual needs of the child within the context of his area of responsibility and with awareness that he is part of a collective treatment effort. All contribute to a child's well-being and development. Thus, the child care worker's contribution encompasses his varied tasks related to living together. The teacher contributes by conveying knowledge of subject matter, developing the child's mastery and skills in educational areas and providing additional opportunities for positive identification. The caseworker or therapist helps the child achieve greater self-understanding.

This description of allocating specialized functions to different disciplines sounds like parcelling out parts of a child among a number of specialists. This is not intended. It would be unrealistic and incorrect. Everyone involved in a continuous relationship with a child must not lose sight of the *wholeness* of the individual. While exercising his particular role, the child care worker, caseworker, teacher and recreation worker must do so in the context of the child's total personality and his interrelated needs. This is stressed in staff training, supervision and integration conferences. It requires continuous communication among the members of the residential treatment team. Because many people are involved in a child's residential life, integration is not easily achieved. This is especially true in large residential settings where the ratio of staff per child is low, relationships between the disciplines are not close, and scheduling is not flexible. Small residential treatment centers, generously staffed, are more likely to achieve a higher degree of integration.

There are residential treatment models that limit the number of persons involved in a child's daily life. For example, the psychoeducateur model developed in Montreal integrates a number of functions in one professional. The psychoeducateur becomes the key person in a child's life, encompassing four disciplines—child care, counselling, education, recreation—as well as coordination of any other services that may be required.

This calls for a highly competent, dedicated, educated and experienced professional. Training of the psychoeducateur, which includes field work as well as academic subjects, takes three to four years in the School of Psychoeducation in the University of Montreal (Guindon, 1973, pp. 27-32).

REFERENCES

ADLER, JACK, "Concepts and Principles in Residential Treatment of Disturbed Children." *Child Welfare,* Vol. 47, No. 9, 1968, pp. 519-523,

GUINDON, JEANNINE, "The Psychoeducateur Training Program." *International Journal of Mental Health,* Vol. 2, No. 1, 1973, pp. 27-32.

MAYER, MORRIS F., "The Group in Residential Treatment of Adolescents." *Child Welfare.* Vol. 51, No. 8, 1972, pp. 482-493.

POLSKY, HOWARD, *Cottage Six: The Social System of Delinquent Boys in Residential Treatment,* New York, Russell Sage Foundation, 1962.

2. The Children

DEVELOPMENTAL STAGES IN CHILDHOOD

Staff working with disturbed or handicapped children should be knowledgeable about normal child development, which provides a point of reference to judge children's deviations from what, in our society, is considered as "normal" and "healthy." The term "normal" does not mean "average" or "sameness" because the developmental stages of childhood involve innumerable nuances and combinations of biological, cultural and social variables. It does imply growth unhampered by physical, emotional and cognitive handicaps.

From the moment of birth, the human organism, with its innate genetic endowment, physical structure and temperamental tendencies, begins a lifelong interaction with environmental forces which surround it. The unfolding of the child's potential is determined by the quality of the nurture he is given and the persons who provide it. In our culture, a loving, secure family environment seems to be the most desirable setting. To enhance healthy development in their children, "parents who allow the unfolding of what is innate, taking care to

14

provide behavioral guidelines and models, do a great deal"
(Akmakjian, 1975, p. 283).

The following outline of normal development is predicated
on the existence of a family environment in which sound nature
(the child's innate endowments) interacts with sustaining
nurture of parenting. The stress is on developing capacities and
behavioral characteristics in the various stages of growth. According to Nichtern (1974, p. 87),

> All behavior is developmentally determined so that it is se-
> quential and identifiable with the stages of life. The early
> reflex movements become the exploratory movements of the
> infant, become the purposeful movements of the young child,
> become the play movements of the older child, become the
> expressive movements of the adolescent, become the work
> movements of the adult. Stages of life are established ar-
> bitrarily by the process of selection and grouping of behavioral
> characteristics, and by the dominance of some features over
> others . . . each of these stages has behavior and communica-
> tion that distinguishes it from the others.

Infancy

During the first half year of life, the infant's muscular, neurological and sensory development accelerates his capacities
to move his body, to sharpen his senses and to react emotionally. He is able to turn his body, to sit and stand up when held,
to see, hear, smell, touch and to express anxiety when separated from his mother. He begins to experiment with people
and objects so that by nine months he is responsive to being
left alone, or to the absence of a familiar toy. He seems to find
comfort in the familiar, clings to his mother and is shy with
strangers. By the end of the first year, he crawls or creeps
about, can stand alone and may be able to take a few steps.
He likes to manipulate toys and utensils. Speech begins to
emerge and he seems to respond to words like "yes" and "no."

Eating and elimination, as well as waking and sleeping, become regulated.

Between 18 and 24 months the infant may walk by himself and push moveable objects. He intensifies his explorations, understands verbal instructions, begins to use a few words and responds cooperatively to the routines of eating, dressing and toilet training. His behavior reflects his self-awareness, his need for his parents and increasing curiosity which is satisfied through his explorations.

Early Childhood (2-5 years)

The two- to three-year-old can walk and run and uses objects appropriately. Most children of this age are toilet trained. He likes to feed himself and to play near other children, but he is not yet ready for collective play. He begins to express himself in sentences, asks questions and likes to listen to stories; his emotional responses become more varied, including expressions of affection, joy, sadness and concern. At four he is active and lively, plays imaginatively, and has fine motor coordination. He can take care of his dressing and grooming needs. He enjoys playing in a peer group and may attach himself to an individual child as his friend. He is more aggressive, assertive and at times negative toward adult authority, which indicates his growing sense of independence. Speech is more extensive and appropriate; he tends to ask innumerable questions.

By five years of age his behavior is well controlled and goal oriented. He accepts rules in games and routines at home. He continues to demonstrate his growing independence by wanting to assume responsibility for personal care and he does not hesitate to venture outside the home to visit with relatives and neighborhood friends. He becomes more aware of differences in size, age, time, strength and sex. He shows an interest in the written word and in expressive arts such as singing, dancing and acting. He becomes preoccupied with family. Boys and girls play games with father and mother roles and play at keeping house. The range of emotional reaction expands, displaying a diversity of feelings and attitudes.

By the end of the fifth year, the child who has grown up in a nurturing, loving and guiding family environment may be considered, according to Erikson (1956), as having satisfactorily achieved a sense of trust, autonomy and initiative. The sense of security in others and in himself developed during the first year of life through his relationship with the most significant person in his life, his mother, who has met his needs with sensitivity and care has conveyed to him that he is worth loving and that others are trustworthy. The sense of autonomy, developed through opportunities for self-expression during the second and third years, is due to encouragement rather than shaming. This has helped him achieve a sense of confidence and a sense that he has control over inner urges. During the next two years, his relationship with his parents encourages a sense of initiative about his explorations and growing awareness of himself as a member of his family.

Late Childhood (6-11 years)

This stage of development, designated by Erikson as "industry versus inferiority," involves children in testing, strengthening and expanding their physical, social, intellectual and emotional capabilities with peers and teachers outside of their immediate family. They are self-reliant but do not hesitate to ask for help when needed. Boys generally get involved in physically strenuous games and sports while most girls tend to be less interested in such activities. Both enjoy creative activities, hobbies, and making things. They readily accept adult authority, rules and routines at home and at school. They find emotional gratification in a diversity of relationships with peer friendships and attachment to adults other than their parents. They enjoy group activities. The characteristic concreteness of early thought is gradually replaced by a capacity for abstract thinking, which facilitates learning. Sexual identification becomes strengthened, with boys preferring the company of boys and their fathers, and girls the company of peers of the same sex and their mothers. The overall rate of growth and development slows down, ushering in a seemingly latent quiescent phase in preparation for the dramatic developments of puberty and adolescence which follow.

Puberty and Adolescence (11-19 years)

Puberty (11-13 years) marks the onset of biological maturation. Hormonal activity results in dramatic changes in physical development. Secondary sexual characteristics include breast development and menstruation in girls; increase in size of penis and testicles, deepening of the voice, appearance of facial hair in boys; and the growth of pubic and underarm hair in both sexes. On the average, girls reach puberty about two years earlier than boys. However, there is a great deal of individual variation. The physical changes are accompanied by emotional and social components which are expressed behaviorally.

Adolescence represents a state of fluidity in all aspects of development. It is characterized by emotional turbulence, ambivalence, impulsivity, search and experimentation. The adolescent's search for identity ("Who am I?" "What do I believe in?" "Where am I going?" "How will I get there?") is reflected in the hairstyles and clothes they wear, fads they follow, heroes they worship, enemies they hate and political and religious causes they follow. According to Nichtern (1974, p. 109):

> Function, behavior and communication are combined and recombined in many different ways, making the adolescent

unpredictable. . . . Their experimentation is physical, social, emotional and intellectual. Their sexual explorations with each other help refine their identity to themselves, while preparing them for the adult roles of marriage partners and parents. Their strong involvement with social groupings and causes serves again to refine their identities to themselves while preparing them to accept the rules and order of the society in which they must live. Their emotionality exposes them to all the nuances of feelings, bringing them to a better awareness of their own needs and those of others. Their intellectual explorations help them toward a selection of a model of work designed to sustain them through later years.

Psychologically, the adolescent is affected by his evolving capacity for abstract thought, the intensification of sexual urges and his identity needs. The horizons of his knowledge expand, sharpening his critical judgment of his immediate surroundings and the greater society which affect his life. His developing sexuality may produce inner tensions experienced as anxiety and guilt because of his emerging sexual feelings. Boys and girls wish for close relationships with members of the other sex, but are fearful of them. Romantic fantasies and "crushes" develop on teachers, star athletes, movie and popular singer idols. The adolescent's search for identity is influenced by family peers and significant (to him) adults other than his parents. In his striving for individuality he alternates between assertion of independence and clinging dependency. His goals are affected by his self-concept, family and peer values, socioeconomic circumstances and educational-vocational opportunities available to him.

Comment

There are many children who have not had the benefit of the type of childhood described above. Among them have been the large number of children of economically poor families who cannot enjoy opportunities for extended play and education because they have had to assume adult responsibilities when still young. Because their mothers had to work, they had to care for themselves or for younger siblings at an early age. To supplement family income many had to work, at a time when their more affluent peers enjoyed the luxury of extended economic dependency. Historically, this has been the prevalent condition of minority group children in America, especially among the black population. They have carried the burden of growing up poor as well as black. Comer and Poussaint (1975, p. 20) state:

> Black children . . . have often assumed the burdens of adulthood at a far too early age. Many have had little of what we call a childhood. In the black world, adolescence starts early in life, and unlike most white youngsters, many black children do not enjoy the luxury of playtime and learning which extends into their late teens.

DISTURBANCE IN CHILDHOOD

Viewed from the perspective of normal child development, the children in residential treatment represent a broad spectrum of deviation. Physically, there may be no apparent difference. Emotionally, intellectually and socially, the differences may be extensive. Appearance and chronological age cannot be considered adequate indices of maturation. The impatient comment, "He is old enough to know better," may be understandable but is not valid. Established achievement level criteria in learning, as well as behavior expectations, do not apply. Judgment of a child's functioning, his capabilities and potentials cannot be established arbitrarily but must be based on knowledge of developmental history and objective observation of overall functioning in the group living situation, school and recreation, as well as on clinical observations in psychiatric and psychological examinations. Such information is helpful to child care workers in dealing with children differentially. One has to begin where a child "is" rather than where we think he "should be." Expectations have to be realistically accompanied by patience, because "progress" may be slow.

Children in residential settings, whether they are classified as abused, dependent, neglected, emotionally disturbed or multiply handicapped, have experienced varying degrees of emotional deprivation. By this we mean a lack of appropriate and adequate environmental and interpersonal experience. The greater the deprivation, the greater the likelihood that the child will be unable to function in accordance with requirements of group living. This is primarily because he is not fully in control of his behavior. Many emotionally deprived children manifest disturbance in relation to reality, impulse (instinctual urge) control, relatedness to others, and thinking. They also manifest extremes in anxiety, anger, aggression and guilt.

Relation to Reality. This involves the ability to perceive accurately the external world and the self. The child or person whose perception of reality is impaired believes that his view of it accurately represents it. Delusions represent an extreme form of misconceiving reality, and hallucinations the extreme in misperceiving it. Severely disturbed children may also be disoriented in time and space. Without supervision and direction they tend to wander off and may get lost, may not get to class or to appointments on time, may be confused about following routines and have difficulty in completing the simplest tasks.

Relatedness. The healthy child reaches out for relationships with others, is able to experience relatedness even in the physical absence of the other person and does not exhibit severe ambivalence. Disturbances in relatedness capacity are expressed in withdrawal from others, instability in maintaining interest in people, or in extreme expressions of love and hate to the same person within a very brief interval. Children who have difficulty in relating to others seem to lack the sense of basic trust derived from experiences during the first years of life. "The amount of trust derived from earliest infantile experience depends on the quality of maternal relationship rather than the quantity of goods or demonstrations of love" (Erikson, 1956, p. 220). According to Erikson, mothers create a sense of trust in their children by behavior which "in its quality, combines sensitive care of the baby's needs and a firm sense of personal trustworthiness within the trusted framework of their cultures and life-styles" (Erikson, 1956, p. 221).

Impulsivity. The healthy child develops increasing control of his inner impulses. He is able to tolerate frustration and postpone gratification. The disturbed child is not capable of doing so. His behavior may range from an inability to sit still for any length of time to destructive outbursts, attacks on others, or temper tantrums; or he may be self destructive. There may also be inappropriate emotional expressions and inappropriate thinking.

Thinking Disorder. The thought patterns of many disturbed children and the intellectually handicapped show a tendency to *concreteness* which represents lack of development or an arrest in thought organization. This requires of a child care worker an approach which will facilitate communication through simple and, if necessary, repeated instructions, and by breaking down a complex task into its constituent parts.

Anxiety

Anxiety expresses itself in an excess of tension, restlessness, and undirected movements. It is a state of feeling generated by instinctual urges when they are not satisfied by the environment. In infancy, when gratification is lacking, the child reacts with crying and bodily dysfunction. Years later, if anxiety develops into a state designated as neurotic anxiety, the extreme emotional and physical reaction to disturbing stimuli may have little connection to the actual objects or situations that evoke it. It is no longer a fear reaction to a real danger but a state of fear of the unknown.

Normally, children either cope with threatening circumstances by learning to overcome the danger, sometimes asking for help, or avoid it by seeking satisfaction elsewhere. They cope with inner anxiety by developing defense mechanisms (see Appendix for definitions), reenacting it in play activities and fantasy. Some children may develop phobias or compulsions. There may also be regression and denial.

In children whose ego development* is highly impoverished, anxiety leads to a breakdown of inner controls, resulting in panic, flight or uncontrollable aggression. Redl and Wineman (1951, p. 96) describe the former as "total flight and avoidance, in which an otherwise pleasure promising activity is abandoned in panic or avoided in the future, if even mild anxiety or fear elements are present"; the latter as "ferocious attack and diffuse destruction, when whatever is in reach, or whoever is near becomes the immediate object of attack, or where the children tear off on a binge of general wild behavior and destruction in a more diffuse way." Such children do not respond easily, if at all, to residential treatment in large settings. They require a great deal of individual attention and highly skilled staff. For example, during almost a year of intensive treatment effort, Ronnie could not involve himself in a closely significant relationship with any staff member. At the age of 9, when he was admitted to the residential treatment

---

* According to psychoanalytic theory the ego, one of the three components of the psychic structure whose prime function is the perception and adaptation to the physical and social environment, inhibits the expression of instinctual drives.

center, he had already failed in 32 foster homes. He repulsed all who attempted to work with him. He threw stones at staff, fought with his peers and ran away. The slightest frustration set off wild rage and assertive behavior. He had to be transferred to a hospital.

Anger and Aggression

Anger and aggression have positive as well as negative connotations. Anger has value in mobilizing a person to act against a realistic danger, hurt or injustice. Aggressiveness is valued in our culture as assertiveness, determination and ambition.

As a consequence of severe or chronic frustration, however, anger may lead to hostile feelings and to aggressive and destructive actions against the object or situation that evokes the painful feelings. It may be turned against the self, producing depression, proneness to accidents, physical illness, and, in extreme cases, destruction of the self through suicide. It may be displaced onto weaker or more vulnerable persons. A child growing up in a family atmosphere where anger and aggression are common modes of expression and interaction will most likely identify with such patterns and reenact them whereever he may be.

In disadvantaged, poverty-ridden families, the consequences of prejudice and discrimination are experienced as deprivation of basic necessities and comforts, low social status, feelings of inadequacy and low esteem, helplessness and hopelessness. Under the burden of extreme frustration which cannot successfully be expressed against the environmental forces which produce it, adults in a family may displace their anger and hostile feelings onto each other and their children. Many troubled parents, especially fathers, may have little love and tender sentiments left to convey to their children. As a result of tension and impatience, they may resort to controlling their children through physical punishment. This tends to weaken emotional bonds and hinders positive identification within the family. It also affects superego or conscience development in their children. This results in weak controls against impulse expression (McKinley, 1964, p. 58). Many such children become delinquent. Some may even become "children who hate" and as a consequence of their destructive aggression they soon become "children nobody wants." Their rehabilitation is extremely difficult because they have severe disturbance and maldevelopment of their "control system" (Redl and Wineman, 1951, pp. 21-28).

Guilt

Guilt is associated with conscience or, in psychoanalytic terminology, the superego. "Conscience represents the mental mechanisms that guide and assist the individual in inhibiting himself from performing acts that are unacceptable to significant figures in his environment. The feelings an individual experiences when he performs, or is tempted to perform, such unacceptable acts is guilt" (Gardner, 1973, p. 125). The superego develops through the internalization of parental prohibitions which ultimately become the unconscious censors of unacceptable thoughts or acts, as well as through identifications with parents and other significant persons in one's life. Their characteristics, standards and values are also internalized and guide future attitudes and behavior.

Guilt has a positive value in regulating social living. When it is excessive or insufficient, it results in maladaptive behavior. Both are in evidence among children in residential treatment. In cases of excessive sense of guilt, a child may suffer from anxiety because he may anticipate retaliation or retribution for angry thoughts or hostile feelings. He may blame himself for misfortunes, accidents, illness or death of loved ones with no basis in reality. He may seek relief by repressing his feelings, by displacing his anger, by developing phobias or compulsions which in symbolic form represent his inner conflicts. He may become depressed or seek punishment for his imagined sins or misdeeds by provoking others to anger and even to physical attack or abuse.

An underdeveloped conscience results in lack or deficiency of guilt feelings. It may be a consequence of impairment in ego development or a result of faulty identifications. When inner urges are not adequately controlled, a child is driven to behave in ways which are unacceptable to others or contrary to established norms or expectations. He may strike out physically, destroy others' belongings, steal, set fires, etc. When lack of guilt is due to identifiication with antisocial values, the child, acting in conformity with his life experience and family or peer expectation, does not feel he is doing anything wrong. He is behaving in accordance with an acceptable life-style which profits from antisocial activity.

Ben exemplified this type of youngster. He was an only child who was reared by a delinquent mother. His father, who was deceased, had been in prison. His was not a poor disadvantaged family; its life-style was delinquent. During the two years of attempted treatment, Ben's mother was uncooperative and encouraged the boy's delinquencies both in the institution and during home visits. He conformed superficially and after his discharge he, in partnership with his mother, became a dealer in drugs. They became affluent and ended up in prison.

Antisocial behavior may also be a consequence of growing up in disadvantaged, economically and socially deprived families and neighborhoods. Many react against their condition by rejecting prevailing social norms and moral values, are antagonistic to them and feel no sense of guilt when they violate them. This was true of Jim during his first year in residential treatment. He made life difficult for his cottage staff and teachers from the moment of his admission. He talked back and was insulting to his child care workers, ignored his teachers and bullied the other children in his cottage and classes. "We can't get through to him! We don't understand him! He is getting us angry!" were frequently heard complaints.

When one considered Jim's background, his behavior was not surprising. Jim was only 12 years old but he had been involved in aggressive and antisocial behavior for years. He had been expelled from school, roamed the streets and was a leader of a delinquent gang. He distrusted adults and felt comfortable with peers only when he could dominate and control them. He seemed to have adopted a style of life characterized by antisocial values and defiance of authority. Jim seemed to behave as if he had brought his previous environment with him. This was a distortion of reality because Jim's cottage living situation was entirely different from his conflict ridden, disorganized home, broken by his father's desertion. Neither was his cottage peer group equivalent to his neighborhood delinquent gang. However, it was Jim's "psychological" reality based on pathological family experiences and deprivation. It seemed that Jim could not be expected to readily give up his characteristic pattern of relating to others and that he would probably resist the institution's encroachment on his accustomed way of life. An essential and initial task was to help the adults who lived and worked with him anticipate, understand and not be provoked by his behavior. This was successfully achieved and Jim eventually gave up his delinquent lifestyle.

Childhood Schizophrenia

Among the very disturbed children referred for residential treatment, those diagnosed as "childhood schizophrenic" (see Appendix) exhibit highly atypical behavior. Because of inner and environmental factors they are unable to adapt to reality requirements of social living. They become frightened and bewildered. They require a therapeutic environment which provides "corrective socialization" (Goldfarb et al., 1969). This implies that:

> The major treatment of the schizophrenic child consists of assisting him, through carefully considered adjustments in his environment, to close up the interstices in his maturation. In other words, treatment must stimulate and reinforce the development of essential adaptive functions which he does not have and strengthen those functions which he already possesses. The therapeutic agents capable of the most immediate impact on the children in this process need not be the psychiatrists and the social workers, as they are conventionally pictured in child guidance, but the child care workers and teachers who are major factors in the child's daily institutional life (Goldfarb et al., 1969, p. 9).

The therapeutic milieu may have to be supplemented by medication to control symptomatic behavior, and by psychotherapy to help the child resolve anxiety evoking conflicts.

Mildly Retarded

These intellectually retarded children may have multiple handicaps, including a combination of mental retardation, neurological deficits and emotional disturbance. Lacking elementary knowledge and skills, they are anxious, suspicious and defensive. Throughout their lives they may have been told by their families, teachers and peers that they were inept, "dumb" and lazy. If they have evoked impatience and low expectations in learning, self-care and social relationships, they may have been neglected. Others may have been overprotected and given little incentive to learn.

Communication with these children may pose problems for child care workers. Their cognitive deficits, expressed in the form of perceptual and language disorders, affect their capacity both to comprehend and to respond appropriately. This tends to evoke negative responses from others. For example, child care workers may interpret the behavior of a child with a language disability as evidence of negativism or "laziness" whenever he does not respond in accordance with expectations, as parents and teachers may have done prior to his placement. His perceptual problems are not readily recognized as responsible for his clumsiness or lack of responsiveness. He may be criticized as "stupid," or even punished for being willfully noncompliant. Adult feelings of hopelessness and helplessness are communicated, reinforcing the child's sense of inadequacy and worthlessness.

The mentally retarded child is a traumatized child because of the chronic rejection he has experienced as a consequence of negative and hostile adult and peer reactions to his inability to meet performance expectation. He is distrustful because he has not experienced a sense of basic trust in his relationships with others. Acceptance of him as a whole child with handicaps conveys a positive attitude that he is worthy of help and that he is likeable. This contributes to the development of a sense of confidence that he can master required tasks (Adler and Finkel, 1976).

The Aggressive Adolescent

Disturbed, aggressive, violence-prone, delinquent-oriented adolescents present special problems for child care workers. As a group they are difficult to live with, work with, and rehabilitate. Most are in placement as a consequence of antisocial acts which brought them to the attention of Family Courts. They are adjudicated as either "juvenile delinquents" or "persons in need of supervision." The former refers to offenses by children under 16 years of age which would be

considered crimes if committed by adults; the latter refers to
boys under 16 and girls under 18 who are beyond the control
of their parents or some other authority because they are in-
corrigible, ungovernable, habitually delinquent or truant from
school. These are legal designations. The label "delinquent,"
which by definition is "guilty of a fault or misdeed," implies
an accusation rather than a description. Such children and
youths generally evoke adult anger and hostility rather than
concern and sympathy. The fact that society fosters delinquency, indirectly or unintentionally, by doing very little about
conditions such as slums, poverty, discrimination and family
disorganization which bred delinquency is frequently dis-
regarded.

Juvenile delinquency is understandably irksome to adult
society. It is wasteful of a community's human and material
resources. Children's antisocial and destructive acts may indicate that something is wrong in their lives. It is often their cry
for help and rescue from intolerable life situations. If society
does not respond with understanding and constructive efforts
to ameliorate conditions which generate their frustrations, delinquency will flourish (Adler, 1966). The categorization of
"juvenile delinquent" tends to stereotype large numbers of
children and youth, de-emphasizing that each is an individual
with a life experience of his own. As a group they represent
a wide range of disturbance.

The principal characteristic juvenile delinquents seem to
have in common is lack of a wholesome family environment.
In the physically deteriorated neighborhoods where the economically and socially disadvantaged reside, harsh conditions
of family life contribute to increased family disorganization,
interpersonal conflict and development of emotional difficulties. Destructive parental attitudes and behavior, whether expressed in direct, overt rejection through abuse and hostile
attitudes or in the form of inconsistent, confused parenting,

lack of adult direction or overindulgence, contribute to childhood confusion, mistrust, conflicts, rejection of society's ethics and values, and the development of antisocial traits and delinquent behavior.

In relatively affluent communities, the emotionally disturbed child or youth may act out his disturbance in destructive ways. Groups of these boys and girls constitute the disruptive, destructive, vandalizing groups present in every suburban community. In recent decades, this has been an increasing phenomenon in so-called middle-class and wealthy neighborhoods and suburbs of our cities. Although the official statistics indicate a much higher delinquency rate among the underprivileged and the low status families who populate marginal and deteriorated neighborhoods and city slums, juvenile delinquency is not the monopoly of the lower socioeconomic classes of our society.

Another neglected element in evaluating the aggressive and disturbed adolescent is his underlying insecurity in forming close relationships with others. Aggression, impulsivity, hostility and destructiveness may be distinguishing traits of delinquent adolescents as a group, but these are not categorically their all-encompassing or exclusive characteristics. Rorschach examinations of the boys in the Glueck studies (Glueck and Glueck, 1950) indicated that the delinquent boys as a group showed a higher incidence of feelings of isolation than the non-delinquent boys. Thus, the individual delinquent's extroverted, aggressive acts may, figuratively speaking, represent only the exposed parts of the "iceberg" of his personality. The individual may camouflage emotional factors such as insecurities and inhibitions in interpersonal relations by behaving aggressively and destructively and by being defiant of adult authority. A study of an adolescent boys' group at the Hawthorne Cedar Knolls School (Adler, 1965), a residential treatment center for emotionally disturbed children, resulted in similar findings, indicating that these emotionally disturbed and, for the most part, delinquent-oriented boys had experienced extensive difficulties within their homes, schools and communities. As a group, they tended to be isolated and inhibited in their capacity for close personal relationships.

From the point of view of rehabilitation objectives, a residential facility should provide children with opportunities for social relationships which would serve to counteract previous destructive interpersonal experiences, and make available the social and psychological nourishment necessary for mature personality development. There are youngsters, however, who are so extensively damaged in their capacity to trust that it is unlikely they will be able to respond to efforts by the staff to involve them in positive relationships. Perhaps because of lack in the current state of knowledge, even the most sophisticated residential treatment center cannot undo or repair the emotional damage some of these children have suffered. This will require additional research and development of more effective treatment methods. This failure may also be due in part to the fact that residential facilities attempting to rehabilitate the aggressive, violence-prone adolescent do not have sufficient clinical services, special education and child care staff to serve the children's needs. Greater community commitment will be needed, together with legislative funding, in order to develop the necessary residential treatment services.

Child care workers are very much aware of the difficulties these violence-prone children represent in group living. The frustrations they impose on other children and on staff can be extreme and at times unbearable. There can develop a sense of hopelessness about their potential for change and a sense of helplessness about one's capacity to be helpful. The child care worker should not expect of himself more than he can possibly give. If there is failure, he is not to blame. If there is a burden of guilt, it belongs among the social forces and circumstances of life which contributed to the development of such severely damaged personalities. A collective communal effort is required to prevent the perpetuation of conditions that produce such children and to protect society from their violence while developing more effective rehabilitation programs.

Violence-Prone Youth

The extremely violent adolescent is relatively rare in current residential treatment programs. However, such youths, including those committing homicide, appear to be increasing in number. They are mentioned here because their background, attitudes and behavior, described by King (1975, pp. 134-145), are similar in many respects to the violence-prone youth in residential settings who present serious management problems for child care workers. Their family situations were full of turmoil and instability. The children were witness to parental fights and were frequent objects of adult abuse; fear was pervasive. Their parents were inconsistent and ineffective. All of these youths were distrustful, expecting insult and injury from everyone. To counteract a sense of vulnerability in social situations, they were ready to attack first. Their primary concern was the satisfaction of their needs without any consideration for others. Anyone who did not give in to their wishes was viewed as a depriving and hostile object that had to be demolished.

They were all severely retarded in reading and language skills. This handicapped their thinking, comprehension, and verbal communication. Their educational deprivation made them defensive about learning. Their capacity to think abstractly and to understand social concept was very limited. Their total reliance on subjective feelings in coping with their environment resulted in impulsive acts and misperception of other people's feelings, behavior and motives. Their reactions, hostile and aggressive in nature, were a prevalent mode of behavior in social situations. If their behavior was questioned, they tended to react with provocative terseness such as, "Who, me?"; "Get off me!"; "Fuck you!"; "Make me!"; "I dare you!", etc. Their manner provoked anxiety, anger and rejection; the violence they emanated generated counter-violence feelings.

This profile is familiar to child care workers responsible for the care of violence-prone (but not necessarily homicidal) youth. The frustration they impose on peers and staff can be extreme. The presence of one or more such youngsters in a cottage group may at times become unbearable because of the fear they generate and the disruption they are capable of creating. They seem to cling desperately and stubbornly to accustomed patterns of behavior, resisting staff efforts to involve them in relationships and in education. Thus they frustrate the objectives of rehabilitation—attempts to help them overcome distrust of social relationships, to develop mastery skills to enhance a sense of confidence they lack, to sublimate destructive energies into constructive endeavor, and to experience a sense of success in achievement rather than failure.

It is therefore not surprising that many child care workers develop a sense of hopelessness about such youngsters. What is more difficult to bear is the feeling of helplessness—of not being effective in helping them change. Some workers question their capacities; others may even blame themselves. This is unrealistic. These adolescents apparently require more than is available today in the most sophisticated residential treatment centers. Additional research will be required to develop more effective treatment approaches. Additional funding is essential to provide existing residential programs with a higher ratio of well trained child care and clinical personnel, special education, vocational training and intensive aftercare services. Most important is a concerted effort to eliminate the destructive socioeconomic conditions which perpetuate the type of family and neighborhood environments which produce such severely damaged personalities.

Psychiatric Diagnoses

Generally, children in residential treatment centers have been examined psychiatrically and their disturbance diagnosed. The diagnosis represents a description of a specific configuration of mental disorders within the general system of psychiatric classification. There are recognizable risks in diagnostic "labeling" because of the fluidity of the child's personality. However, a clinical diagnosis facilitates understanding and formulation of treatment plans. For example, whereas "psychoneuroses" implies the need for resolution of internalized conflicts through acquisition of insight by means of psychotherapy, a schizophrenic patient requires therapeutic support in daily living based on reality rather than evocation of psychological insights. When classifying children as "schizophrenic," "character disorder," "neurotic," etc., we should keep in mind that "each child whatever his symptom is a distinct individual with his own . . . pattern and range of potentialities" (Murphy, 1974, p. 14).

In child care work there are innumerable situations where differential approaches are indicated on the basis of diagnostic understanding of the children involved. For example, four children during a meal may refuse to eat vegetables. When the worker insists, they all get upset but express it differently. The psychotic child may become extremely anxious and if forced may be propelled into a psychotic episode. This is because he may view this type of food as a harmful substance which will poison him if he eats it. The worker who insists on it may then be viewed as a poisoner, and the possibility of continued trusting relationships with him is destroyed. The second child, with a history of mother-child conflict, may associate vegetables with traumatic experiences related to forced feeding by his mother. If pressured he may have a temper tantrum, repeating previous reactions to his mother. The third child, who does not like vegetables because he doesn't like their taste, may ask to be excused from eating them. The fourth child, with manipulative tendencies, will want to skip vegetables in order to get to the dessert. He will attempt either to trade off to another child or to manipulate the worker out of pressuring him to eat them. Diagnostic understanding will suggest that the first child cannot be forced; it will take a long time before he feels secure enough to trust an adult's offer and eat this food. The second child will need time to dissociate the worker's behavior from emotions associated with early feeding experiences. The value of vegetables can be discussed with the third child, possibly to the point of convincing him he should try them even though at this time he doesn't like the taste. Manipulative behavior by the fourth child should not be permitted. The dessert could be withheld without inordinate emotional or physical harm to him since other food is still available to him.

Routines of daily living need not be changed for each child on the basis of his diagnosis. However, children require some degree of individualization. A child care worker should not hesitate to ask for clarification by clinical personnel if a diagnostic statement is unclear and if he is not sure of its implications in dealing with a particular child. For detailed descriptions of psychiatric diagnostic classifications, consult Appendix A.

REFERENCES

ADLER, JACK, "The Aggressive Delinquent Oriented Adolescent in Residential Treatment," *Child Welfare*, Vol. 48, No. 3, 1969, pp. 142-147.

ADLER, JACK, "Transfer of Interpersonal Behavior Among Emotionally Disturbed Adolescents in Residential Treatment." Ed.D. thesis, (unpublished), Teachers College, Columbia University, 1965.

ADLER, JACK, and FINKEL, WILLIAM, "Integrating Remedial Methods into Child Care Practice." *Child Care Quarterly*, Vol. 5, No. 1, 1976.

AKMAKJIAN, HAIG, *The Natural Way to Raise a Healthy Child*. New York, Praeger, 1975.

COMER, JAMES P. and POUSSAINT, ALVIN F., *Black Child Care*. New York, Simon and Schuster, 1975.

ERIKSON, ERIK H., *Childhood and Society*. New York, Norton, 1956.

GARDNER, RICHARD A., *Understanding Children*. New York, Jason Aronson, 1973.

GLUECK, SHELDON and GLUECK, ELEANOR, *Unravelling Juvenile Delinquency*. Cambridge, Mass., Harvard University Press, 1950.

GOLDFARB, WILLIAM, MINTZ, IRVING, and STROOCK, CATHERINE W., *A Time to Heal: Corrective Socialization, a Treatment Approach to Childhood Schizophrenia*. New York, International Universities Press, 1969.

KING, CHARLES H., "The Ego and the Integration of Violence in Homicidal Youth." *American Journal of Orthopsychiatry*, 45(1), January, 1975, pp. 134-145.

MCKINLEY, GILBERT D., *Social Class and Family Life*. New York, Free Press, 1964.

MURPHY, BARCLAY LOIS, *Growing Up in Garden Court*. New York, Child Welfare League of America, 1974.

NICHTERN, SOL, *Helping the Retarded Child*. New York, Grossett & Dunlap, 1974.

REDL, FRITZ and WINEMAN, DAVID, *Children Who Hate*. New York Free Press, 1951.

3. Tasks

THE CHILD CARE WORKER'S
ROLE AND FUNCTION

"Life with children" encompasses the child care worker's tasks. Therapeutic care is his function; rearing children of stress is his preoccupation. He is not a parent, but exercises parental functions; he is not a teacher, but educates; he may not be a recreation worker, but he plays with children and organizes leisure time activities; he is not a housekeeper, but has responsibility for orderly functioning of the children's living environment. In all of his tasks, the child care worker has opportunities to contribute to healthy development of children. These tasks include the following (Beker, 1970, pp. 3-4):

1. He participates in daily living routines. Throughout the day, from waking to bedtime, the child care worker guides the children in establishing and maintaining health promoting and socially desirable habits regarding personal hygiene, grooming, mealtime behavior, leisure time activities and interaction with peers and adults.

2. He supports the maintenance of standards regarding physical nurture such as adequate diet, clothing, leisure time activities, pleasant, attractive and comfortable living conditions.
3. He provides a sense of security and safety for each child in group living by assuring protection from being hurt physically or abused emotionally.
4. He is concerned about children's health needs. Under medical or nursing supervision, he may care for a child who is ill, give first aid and dispense medication.
5. He encourages and, as necessary, assists children in their formal education by consulting with teachers, helping with homework and conveying a positive attitude toward learning.
6. Through participation in maintaining physically attractive and clean housing conditions, he helps children develop constructive attitudes toward work as well as pride in their living environment.
7. He is involved in planning with the children the organization of leisure time activities. He encourages participation in group games and development of game skills.
8. Through objective observation, sensitivity and a readiness to meet children's emotional needs, he conveys a sense of empathy and encourages a trusting relationship between children and himself.
9. He interprets to children the institution's policies and requirements.
10. He consults, shares information and participates with members of other disciplines in planning and evaluation conferences on the children in his group.

The child care worker represents authority as well as reality for the children who find it difficult to cope with demands of daily living, have problems in relating to others, and cannot control inner impulses which strive for immediate gratification. The day's routines may become an arena of conflict if children and workers are in antagonistic roles.

Throughout the day the child care worker is expected to cope with children's maladaptive behavior with understanding and firmness, with appropriate responses related to a particular child's personality, his needs and treatment objectives. Each interaction between a worker and a child may have immediate therapeutic significance and long-term implications. To live with a group of disturbed children and to cope with the turbulence of their emotions and their resistances, while at the same time meeting the demands of a structured milieu, administrative expectations and set schedules, are not easy tasks. They require firmness and patience, organizational skills, competence, confidence and a capacity to "give" to children without any assurance of reciprocity, or of appreciative responses.

Since many of the children find it difficult to return the love, care and concern of a dedicated adult, it is not unusual to hear a child care worker express disappointment that his interest and devotion are not "appreciated" by a child. This is not a question of appreciation but a manifestation of the child's disturbance. Such a child may not have experienced the human nurture which promotes trust in others. He may fear human closeness and avoid attachments because he anticipates rejection. His particular behavior may be a defense against closeness with another person. No matter how pathetic, detached, resistive or hostile a child may appear, he may want to be loved and protected by adults. His resistance and fears may be ultimately overcome by patience and understanding. However, the process of achieving trust may be lengthy and difficult with many children and never realized with some. Mere "sympathy" for these children does not suffice. Empathic sensitivity based on genuine feelings and caring is required. Emotionally disturbed children with their supersensitivity are masters at spotting devious motivations of adults. If interest in them is not genuine, they will become aware of it very quickly. The child care worker must be concerned for the whole child and not simply a segment of him which may be to his liking.

A degree of self-awareness in this respect can be productive. It is a most valuable asset for a child care worker to be able to see himself objectively, to be aware of his feelings and of the responses that the children's behavior evoke in him, and to be capable of perceiving objectively how the children view him. This is especially important because, as a closely significant person in the children's lives, the worker may become a target of ambivalent feelings and misplaced emotions. Ambivalence refers to the coexistence of opposite or antithetical emotions, attitudes or wishes toward the same person or situation. Generally, only one aspect of the feelings is conscious or partly conscious, the other remaining unconscious, viz., love and hate toward the same person or situation (*A Psychiatric Glossary*, 1964, p. 11).

The child care worker not only represents a giving person but, like a parent, is also a controlling adult. He demands conformity to the rules and regulations which comprise the structure of the residence. In exercising parental functions he may stimulate transference behavior (Adler, 1973). Transference is defined as the "unconscious transfer to others of feelings and attitudes which were originally associated with important figures (parents, siblings) in one's early life" (*A Psychiatric Glossary*, 1964, p. 76). A child care worker's familiarity with a particular child's tendencies to replicate or repeat earlier patterns of relationships in his interactions with adults, as well as with peers, may help the worker understand when the child's behavior toward himself represents transference manifestations. This may diminish the probability of his being drawn into the child's projected transference roles and avoid inappropriate reactions on his part. The sense of frustration and resentment experienced from being a persistent object of a child's irrational behavior can be great. Angry or even hostile counterreaction is understandable, even though its consequences for the child and the child-worker relationship may be harmful. If the child-care worker's reaction to the child is subjective or impulsive, it may be considered inappropriate. It may also represent countertransference behavior.

Wolstein has referred to transference and countertransference as "bipolar or reciprocal phenomena" (Wolstein, 1954, p. 196). In psychoanalysis, countertransference refers to anxiety aroused in the analyst by his patient, and may involve both positive and negative feelings, irrational dislike or overidentification, linking the patient to some significant person in the analyst's life. If such reactions can occur in trained and "analyzed" professionals such as psychoanalysts, they can be expected to happen in relationships between a child care worker and a child. In intensive, emotion-laden situations, a child's behavior may evoke reactions tinged by either positive or negative transference. The worker's highly subjective response, triggered by a child's behavior, may represent a link to his own past.

This aspect of the child care worker's interaction with the children cannot be avoided; however, it can be minimized. The greater the awareness of his own reactions to children's transference behavior, the less likely will the child care worker be to respond in countertransference terms. Thus, a worker may feel upset by a child's hostile reactions to his acts of "giving" or "helping" which represent his interest and his "caring" for the child. However, he is less likely to react with anger and hostility when he understands the basis of the child's responses. Through his residential treatment experience, such a child will, hopefully, begin to view his child care workers as individuals in their own right rather than in transference terms.

Children's judgments of adults can be highly perceptive. Adult failings cannot be concealed from them. When they feel free to express their observations, they are generally objective. This was dramatically illustrated in a group therapy session of a group of adolescent boys who behaved disruptively and hostilely toward a child care worker. The following notes, taken by one of the group leaders, summarize the children's reactions:

Listed below are some of the criticisms which the group articulated in relation to the cottage father:

One was his impulsivity, in that he was quick to lose his temper when frustrated by the group. He often made threats which he did not even intend to carry out and which were not qualitatively or quantitatively appropriate to the incidents which evoked them. They were critical of his lack of consistency, so that the boys were unable to anticipate in any given situation whether his behavior would be similar to what it was in a similar situation previously, or would be entirely different. They complained bitterly that this inconsistency paralleled the inconsistencies which they had experienced from their own parents at home.

They viewed the cottage father as weak, having no "back-bone" and this reflected upon his adequacy as an adult after whom they were expected to pattern their own responses. He did not give of himself generously. When he "gave," in terms of material giving, recognition, etc., there was always an underlying desire on his part to exact some kind of price from the boys to whom he did the giving. He wanted gratefulness from them, or exchange of favors, etc. This signified to them that his giving was calculated and therefore not real. Another objection was that they expected an adult to be understanding of their pathology and idiosyncracies, and he was not. This was interpreted by them to represent a genuine lack of understanding in a person working with disturbed kids. Finally, they felt that he played favorites, and also that he was rigid and vindictive—rigid in the sense that they had the feeling that the rules were more important than the children for whom the rules were intended, and vindictive because he felt obliged to retaliate whenever anything was done which reflected upon his power or prestige. They were able to split him off from the established structure of the school. He was capricious in making his own rules relating to conduct in the cottage, despite the fact that he referred to the administration demands upon him as a means of bolstering what authority he had.

The boys correctly assessed their worker's insecurities about exercising authority and resented his attitudes which seemed to be defensive.

Lemay (1974, pp. 7-8) suggests a number of basic attitude requirements for child care workers who work with children with a precarious adaptation to reality.

1. Acceptance and respect for each child as he is without value judgments.
2. Attitude of self-awareness.
3. Attitude of involvement. The worker accepts the reality of living and working with disturbed children without losing his objectivity and orientation to reality.
4. Attitude of evaluation. Through objective observation of daily behavior, the worker becomes aware how a child perceives and deals with reality situations. Through the worker's relationship with the child, he is helped to replace maladaptive functioning with behavior appropriate to reality.

5. Striving for continuity in the relationship with a child during his placement. This involves long-term commitment and regularity of presence.
6. Attitude of genuineness. This emphasizes the fundamental role in a relationship where both transference and countertransference elements have to be recognized where possible.
7. Individualization. The disturbed child must not be viewed as a "category" or stereotype of maladjustment. Each child is a unique personality who has to be understood in terms of his total life experience, the mechanisms of his behavior and his defenses against meaningful relationships with others.

The above "requirements" are of concern because they demand a great deal of a child care worker. They may be considered "unrealistic" or as "ivory tower idealism" and therefore unattainable. We believe that they are meant to be goals to work toward rather than rigid standards of expectation for all. When viewed as conceptual guidelines they are useful objectives, and as important in the education of child care workers as the specifics of daily child care management. The stark realities of the child care worker's job are not minimized by conceptual frameworks, nor by professional goals. We are well aware that the strains of living with disturbed children can at times be overwhelming to the most experienced of workers. The children's impulsivity, self-centeredness, manipulativeness and provocations can frustrate the most patient temperament and evoke anger from the most tolerant. The process of achieving a high degree of effectiveness involves knowledge, development of skills and self-awareness. It cannot be an immediate expectation. Learning opportunities have to be made available in an atmosphere of support; mistakes which are inevitable need to be tolerated. Individual supervisory conferences, peer group discussion and seminars should encourage frankness in expressing feelings and opinions. It is particularly important for a worker to feel sufficiently secure in his relationships with his supervisor and co-workers to express himself freely. Unless he is able to describe conflict situations that arise during the course of his daily activities frankly, his supervisor will be handicapped in helping him learn from them.

A TYPICAL DAY

The child care worker's tasks involve the children's waking hours, as exemplified by the following example of a schedule in a residential treatment center.

Weekdays

7:30 A.M. - 8:25 A.M.	Wake up, wash and dress, make beds, do room chores such as dust, sweep, bring laundry downstairs.
8:25 A.M. - 9:00 A.M.	Breakfast
9:00 A.M. - 11:55 A.M.	A.M. school session During school hours children have appointments with social workers, remedial teachers; individual tutoring is also done.
11:55 A.M. - 12:00 Noon	Wash up for lunch
12:00 Noon - 1:00 P.M.	Lunch
1:00 P.M. - 3:00 P.M.	P.M. school session
3:00 P.M.	Afternoon snack
3:15 P.M. - 4:45 P.M.	Chores—shoeshining, haircuts, clothing to cleaners, etc.
3:15 P.M. - 4:45 P.M.	Afternoon group meetings for younger children. Participation in group work program.

4:45 P.M. - 5:00 P.M.	Wash up for supper
5:00 P.M. - 5:40 P.M.	Supper
6:00 P.M. - 8:00 or 9:00 P.M.	For intermediate and older children, activities such as arts and crafts, scouts, folk dancing, free play, sports activities in gymnasium, etc.
7:00 P.M.	Showers, for younger children
7:30 P.M.	Evening snack for younger children
8:00 P.M.	Showers, for older children
8:30 P.M.	Evening snack for older children
8:30 P.M. - 10:00 P.M.	Bedtime, depending on age (past 10.00 on discretionary basis when there is no school the next day)

Weekends

8:00 A.M.	Wake up
9:00 A.M.	Breakfast
10:00 A.M. - 4:00 P.M.	Trip program—to points of interest
10:00 A.M. - 4:30 P.M.	Day visits with parents—on scheduled basis, routinely twice monthly on Saturday or Sunday
10:00 A.M. - 5:00 P.M.	Lunch
12:00 Noon - 1:00 P.M.	Older children go off grounds individually or in twos or threes to movies, etc.; free play
5:00 P.M. - 6:00 P.M.	Supper
6:00 P.M. - 8:00 P.M.	Some activities scheduled (with resident staff)
7:00 P.M. - 10:00 P.M.	Snack, showers, bedtime—same as weekdays

The Edenwald School Manual of Policies and Procedures (1973) states:

> This is not a fixed, rigid routine, but rather a "typical" day. Experience has shown that our children need routines and a predictable sequence of events. Actually all human beings need some degree of order, routine, and predictability in their lives. Children who come from disorganized homes where people and events were often unpredictable and whose perceptions of the world are distorted because of their emotional disturbance or perceptual disorders need a strong and clearly perceptible ordering of the sequence of events each day, week, season, and year. On the other hand, human beings are deadened by lives which are excessively routinized. A certain amount of unpredictability and surprise adds spice to life and actually helps a child prepare for the unpredictability of life itself. The institution, therefore, provides a basic framework of routines within which the child will live. It tries through certain programs to add variety, beauty, fun and some unexpectedness to their lives. However, the child care worker is in the most strategic position to provide this necessary element in the lives of the children. He is not only encouraged, but it is part of his responsibility to add variety and surprise to life in the institution. Late privileges, trips, an occasional special treat, a spontaneous activity, special arrangements to see a fine TV program, joking and horseplay with the children—all contribute to making institutional living a livelier and more nearly "normal" experience for them. These are the means for preserving what is whole in the children's personalities and giving them a sense of the fun and delight which should be part of life.
>
> Weekends are not tightly scheduled. There are for most children large blocks of free time with which they are free to do what they want—or do nothing at all.

DAY'S BEGINNING

Anxieties

Waking from a night's sleep may not be a welcome occasion for many disturbed children. The prospect of facing the potential demands of the day evokes anxiety. This is demonstrated by the diversity of waking patterns which confront the child care worker each morning. Some children may respond quickly to his call for rising, others lag behind, and some cannot manage the process of washing and dressing without help. Many children tend to wake up troubled. Some are so anxious about the day's expectations that they seem disoriented in terms of time and place. Sometimes a child, upon awakening, explores parts of his body as if to check whether he is "all there"; some may still be under the influence of frightening dreams; others may be resentful of being wakened from the security of sleep and react hostilely.

Waking

Waking the children requires sensitivity, tolerance, patience and firmness. One might begin the process in an encouraging manner, rousing each one individually, calling out his name or touching him lightly. Children who do not arise quickly may have to be reminded several times. If this is not effective, one can call attention to the institution's rules regarding morning routines. This tends to shift the child's view of the worker as a disturber of his peace to one who reminds him of the requirements that are expected of everyone. It is most important that the worker not compromise established routines. He should persist with firmness but without anger or hostile actions such as turning over a child's bed or spraying him with water—unwholesome punitive methods which have occasionally been used by workers.

If a child complains about not feeling well, he may be actually ill, or it may be a manifestation of anxiety about going to school that day. A child care worker who knows the children well usually knows who is telling the truth and who is feigning. Until this knowledge is certain, arrangements should be made for every child who complains about illness to see a nurse. Persistent manifestations of anxiety should be reported to a child's caseworker. Discussion should be held with any child known to be a manipulator.

Washing and Dressing

Once all the children are awake, the worker faces problems related to washing and dressing. Some children have difficulties in taking care of their grooming. It is not valid to assume that a child who is slow in these activities is purposely "stalling." Some children, while dressing, may slip into daydreaming fantasies. They seem literally suspended in time between such relatively simple acts as putting on one shoe after the other. They need help to speed up the dressing process. The worker may, for example, list the pleasant activities which the child can expect that day. A "counting" game (Whittaker, 1969, p. 124) may be suggested with the worker counting to see how many seconds it takes the child to put on his socks and shoes. On subsequent mornings, he will be encouraged to reduce the time interval. Praise may be offered or a token reward given as positive reinforcement. Some children may actually need a worker's help in getting dressed. This may be a hardship at a time when he is responsible for getting the whole group ready for breakfast; however, teaching a young child to master these skills is very important.

Some children, following awakening, may get involved in masturbatory activity. This should be handled simply by telling the child to "get dressed." If this behavior persists, a plan of action should be developed jointly with the child's caseworker.

Pre-Breakfast Activity

Since children dress at different rates, some will be ready before others. If there are chores, such as making beds or sweeping, to be done these become the focus of the worker's attention. Play activities or TV watching before breakfast may become an issue, especially for those children who have completed their chores and have waiting time before breakfast. TV viewing can become a problem because children may become too involved in a particular program. This can best be handled by telling the children in advance that it is time to get ready for breakfast. Quiet games should be encouraged, while horsing around, disruptive behavior and obvious delaying tactics should not be tolerated. The worker must make it clear that this behavior is not acceptable since it delays the group.

Going off to the dining hall (if breakfast is served centrally) and later to school may involve a struggle about appropriate dress. It is the worker's responsibility to make sure that every child is dressed in accordance with weather conditions. Wearing boots or rubbers in rain and snow is frequently resisted but is necessary if the children are to remain well.

Greater understanding of individual children, of the group as a whole, and of his own reactions can be developed by the child care worker through the observations listed below.

Morning Observations

Individual Child

1. Does he wake easily; or is it difficult to rouse him?
2. Is he overly slow—seemingly "half-awake" or daydreaming?
   a. Does he seem anxious after arising?
   b. Does he seem disoriented regarding time?
   c. Does he examine parts of his body?
3. Does he get through with bathroom duties quickly?

4. Are there problems about washing or grooming?
5. Does he complain he "can't find" items of clothing?
6. Does he dress quickly or require only an occasional reminder?
7. Does he seem to "stall" to create delay for others and/or a power struggle with worker?
8. Is he slow because he is compulsive or perfectionistic about dressing?
9. Does he appropriately ask for help when it is needed?
10. Does he refuse help when it is offered?
11. What does he do after dressing while awaiting the call for breakfast? What is his general mood—quiet, jovial, disruptive, cranky, angry?

Self-awareness questions

1. What is your own mood this morning?
   a. Watchful, pleasant, encouraging, eager to help the children, thus facilitating their own efforts to get ready for the day's activities?
   b. Troubled, moody, angry, impatient with difficult children?
2. Do you react inappropriately to a child's irrational behavior toward you, or do you understand that you may be the object of displaced emotions?
3. Are things well organized to help the children (clothes laid out, bathroom facilities checked and in order, activities planned for those who get ready quickly)?
4. Is "continuity" assured, i.e., have you information from others about the children and their behavior? Is your pattern of routines the same as your co-workers', assuring consistency of approach?

MEALTIME

Emotional Connotation of Food

Food has emotional as well as nutritional significance. *How* one is fed may be more important than *what* is fed. The feelings accompanying a mother's offering of food to her child evoke complementary reactions, resulting in emotional associations with feeding. These may range from feelings of being loved to rejection, pleasure to frustration, tenderness to anger. Withholding of food may be viewed by the child as withholding of love and care. Mealtime experienced in a positive family milieu becomes associated with a sense of family togetherness, sharing of food, conversation and satisfying social interaction. Negatively experienced, it is associated with frustration, loneliness, rivalry, conflict and unpleasantness. Thus, anxieties and conflicts experienced by children during meals may give rise to a spectrum of ambivalent feelings toward food, as well as toward parent figures.

For many children in residence, mealtime in their homes had not been a happy time. They may, therefore, have developed food fads, poor eating habits and other anxieties associated with eating. They tend to perpetuate accustomed mealtime behavior and to transfer negative attitudes felt toward a feeding person, generally from their mothers to child care workers. A child may dawdle, gorge or eat with his fingers, eliciting anger from peers and adults; another may complain about the quality or quantity of food without justification; still another may refuse to eat certain foods or not eat enough. The emotionally deprived child may overeat; the economically disadvantaged child may hoard food. Both deprived children will need reassurance that there is enough for everyone and that "seconds" are available. Limits have to be set for the child who throws food around or grabs the first portion to be served;

the child who is unskilled in the use of utensils will have to be taught.

Routines and Expectations

Institutional routines tend to compensate for a child's immaturities. The very fact that meals are scheduled is an aid in preparing for this event. Children learn that they have to be ready to postpone other activities. They cannot blame the worker's temperament for interrupting what they are doing. It is advisable to remind children to get ready five or ten minutes in advance. They need a period of preparation to make a transition from one set of activities to another. Hyperactive children may have to be reminded still earlier in order to help them "cool down."

Mealtime is an important social event. The physical surroundings should be attractive and comfortable. Disorder conveys to children a lack of caring and respect for them and they will react accordingly. A mess breeds messiness; a depressing atmosphere contributes to restlessness, evokes anxiety and can lead to acting-out behavior.

Seating arrangements are important and should be designated by staff. The location of the worker may have to be flexible. He might sit between two children who easily provoke each other, next to a child who generally initiates conflict situations, or adjacent to one who has difficulty in managing utensils, or who is fearful of eating certain foods or of aggression by peers. Thus the worker may serve in many roles—as buffer, guide, teacher or protector.

Children should be aware of expectations regarding behavior at table. Every child is expected to eat with the group. Shouting, fighting, throwing of food are not allowed. Children cannot leave the table without the worker's permission. Table manners should be stressed since they convey respect for others. Some children are unaware of this and require guidance.

Food should be well prepared and served promptly, quickly and attractively. How it is served and by whom is generally determined by the degree of the children's maturity. Children may pass it or the worker may serve.

Children should be encouraged to assume responsibility during meals. They should learn to pass the food appropriately and to take turns in clearing the table. It is important to prevent disturbances before they start, because once they begin, they affect the whole group. If things get out of hand, it may be advisable to remove the child who is responsible.

Children should neither be deprived of food as punishment nor be forced to eat. Each child has his own capacity and the worker should be able to individualize the children in this respect. A child who has food fads may take some time to get over his anxiety about a phobic food and may need the help of his caseworker to accomplish it. However, the worker must also be aware of manipulation at mealtimes. For example, some children may refuse to eat vegetables or the main course in order to fill up with extra desserts. This should not be permitted.

Plans for the day's leisure time activities may be discussed during mealtime. Story telling or word games with younger children can minimize restlessness while waiting for food.

Observations

The following are suggested guidelines for observation during mealtime:

The Group

1. Do seating arrangements cause problems? Should anyone be moved to another table?
2. Which of the children need assistance with eating, use of utensils, table manners?

3. What is the general mood of the children—friendly, quiet, tense, noisy?
4. What is the atmosphere today? Has something affected the behavior of the children in general or of any child in particular?
5. What complaints are there about the food? Its preparation? Quality? Quantity?
6. Is it possible to talk with the children about problems occurring at mealtimes and to involve them in resolving them? If not, what and who are the obstacles?

Individual Child

1. Note individual patterns of behavior during mealtime:
   a. Does he eat calmly and quietly?
   b. Is he cooperative or does he attempt to provoke you or other children?
   c. Does he snatch food?
   d. Take too much food?
   e. Eat very little?
   f. Eat very slowly?
   h. Steal food?
   i. Throw food?
   j. Use fingers instead of utensils?
2. What are his favorite foods? Does he have food fads? What food does he refuse to eat? If pressured to eat it, how does he react? Does he become agitated, cry, use abusive language, or have a temper tantrum?
3. Is he sociable at the table?
4. Is he fearful?
5. Is he cooperative?
6. What is his mood—content, jovial, depressed, etc.?
7. Does he converse with other children? Does he converse with the worker?
8. Does he try to monopolize the worker's attention?

9. Is he provocative towards the worker? Does he interfere when others try to talk with the worker or with
peers?

10. Does he start fights?

Self-Awareness Questions

1. Does your own mood affect the group atmosphere?
Is the influence positive or negative?
2. Are you impatient with the children? If so, why?
3. Do you like to eat with the children?
4. Do you find mealtime aggravating or pleasant?
5. When the food is not to your liking, do you express
your dissatisfaction in the children's presence? If you
have done so, what has been their reaction?
6. How do you feel towards a child who disrupts mealtimes?
7. What methods do you use to control misbehavior at
mealtime? Are they effective?
8. Are you comfortable conducting a group discussion
about disruptive mealtime behavior?

EDUCATION

The child care worker, not unlike a parent, is closely involved in children's education. He sends a child off to school
and greets him when he returns; he helps with homework;
through contact with teachers and caseworkers, he learns about
the educational achievements or the handicaps of the children
in his group.

Learning Difficulties

Many of the children may have problems at school. Learning
difficulties arise for a number of reasons:

1. Education emphasizes *reality*. The child whose reality testing is impaired will find adaptation to classroom requirements difficult. Anxiety in its varied forms, evoked by reality demands, will interfere with learning.

2. Education involves *relationships*. One learns most easily through loving and trusted adults. Consequently, the child who has not experienced love and trust has an impaired capacity to relate to others. He approaches new relationships with distrust and insecurity. His defenses may range from avoidance to attack; he usually finds it easier to keep a safe distance from significant relationships with his teachers.

3. *Poor impulse control*, a characteristic of many disturbed children, deflects attention from concentration.

4. A child may be handicapped by a *learning disorder* associated with impairment of the central nervous system as a result of brain injury sustained at birth, or through infection, accident, biochemical irregularity, mental deficiency, genetic causes. Or, he may have a *learning disability*, not associated with mental deficiency.

5. Some children may have had a poor educational experience. If they have failed, they bring with them a poor sense of adequacy, a lack of self-confidence, and negative attitudes towards teachers. They may resist education because of fear of exposing their inadequacies.

6. Family and cultural attitudes may also account for lack of educational motivation.

Under optimal conditions residential schooling occurs within an educational program which is integrated with the clinical, as well as the environmental, aspects of the total residential program. Such a school makes demands on children in accordance with their capabilities, which are identified early in the child's residence. If a child is educationally retarded, acceptance of his level of competency is conveyed to him and efforts are made to help him overcome deficiences. Teachers help him compete against himself instead of against others. They assist him in developing skills, beginning with his level of competency and working toward achievement of his potential. Teachers with clinical understanding can convey to the child their understanding of the difficulties which have hindered his learning (Adler, 1963, pp. 219-220).

Child Care Worker's Role

Children in general, and especially disturbed children, cannot be expected to have mature attitudes about the value of education. The children need to feel that the adults around them value learning and take an active interest in their education. This involves provision for study time and a physical setting conducive to study in the cottage, checking homework, visiting classrooms and contact with teachers.

Depending on the relationship he has with a child, the child care worker may be able to counteract insecurities, as well as negative attitudes toward learning, through his expressed interest in the child's education and class functioning, the positive values of education he represents, the understanding he conveys, and the actual help he offers. A child may exert greater effort if the worker shows interest. As he incorporates the worker's values, he may gradually evolve a sense of confidence in himself and begin to view education as an asset instead of an imposition.

Disruptive classroom behavior becomes a concern of child care workers as well as teachers. When it comes to the attention of the worker, he should discuss it with the child. Expressed concern, support of classroom expectations, and disapproval of destructive behavior are in order and can be helpful. However, the worker should not be expected to become a disciplinarian for school related misdeeds, nor the executioner for school prescribed punishment. This remains the responsibility of teacher and school administration.

The Mentally Retarded Child

The child with intellectual handicaps poses special problems for the child care worker. He is distrustful because he has not experienced a sense of basic trust in his relationship with others. He is insecure and fearful of learning because failure rather than mastery has been the fruit of his efforts. He has a sense of hopelessness about his capabilities and strong defenses against exposing himself in learning situations. The worker trying to help such a child faces difficulties and discouragement. A great deal of patience and persistence in pursuing the educational process in which he engages with the child will be necessary. The child may test his patience to the utmost before understanding that the worker's effort is an expression of a genuine desire to help him learn. Acceptance of him as a whole person, even with his handicaps, conveys a positive attitude that he is indeed capable of learning and worth teaching. This may contribute to the development of a sense of confidence that he can master the tasks in which the worker is involved as helper and teacher. Success here will inevitably help in other areas of learning. The child care worker thus becomes an important reinforcer of learning within the total education of the child.

The quality that enables the worker to feel what the child must be experiencing is helpful. Indeed, the more he knows of each child in terms of his cognitive shortcomings, the more capable he will be of putting himself in the child's place, empathizing with him for the embarrassment and shame that he surely feels for his inability to follow instructions. Empathy for the child means an understanding of what it is to be like him. Conveying this understanding can help build rapport with him, the essential ingredient of a relationship through which he may be motivated to learn (Adler and Finkel, 1976).

Observations of Educational Attitudes

1. Does he seem to like school? Is he indifferent to it? Does he dislike it?
2. Is it difficult to get him to go to school. Does he complain about not feeling well, forget his books, dawdle, etc.?
3. Attitude about homework—does he do it efficiently, compulsively, or sloppily? Does he need to be admired? Does he refuse to do it?
4. Does he ask for help with school work? Does he refuse help when offered? Will he accept help but not ask for it?
5. Does he read books, newspapers? Is reading limited to comic books, or does he not read at all?
6. Does he have a special educational or vocational interest or goal?
7. Does he speak favorably of his teachers? Does he like any one in particular? Does he dislike them all?
8. Is he concerned about his school performance? Is he anxious about grades or about taking examinations?

Religious Education

The extent of religious education and religious services in a given setting is determined by the philosophy of the institution, which in turn may be influenced by legal requirements, sectarian affiliation, or board and administrative conviction. The predominant attitude that religious education is necessary for the spiritual development of children, and that religious training is regarded as a parental responsibility, extends to residential care.

Child care workers exert a direct as well as an indirect influence in relation to religious training. They generally accompany children to religious services, are involved in decorating the cottages for holidays and participate in religious celebrations. Indirectly, a child care worker has an even greater impact on children's attitudes because children learn more by example than from instruction. The child care worker who identifies with the religious philosophy and practices of an institution may by his very presence and actions encourage children to do the same. In a nonsectarian institution, a child care worker should not only be familiar with the concepts and practices of the different religions represented by the children in his group, but he also must convey a sense of tolerance for all religions. By doing so, he demonstrates respect for all of the children, regardless of their cultural, ethnic or religious background. He also contributes to the modification of existing prejudices among the children and to the acceptance of differences. The sense of tolerance conveyed helps create an atmosphere of cultural, religious and ethnic pluralism which is the heritage of a democracy.

WORK

Group living provides opportunities for the learning of skills, self-care and social responsibility. Success at work tasks in the cottage may give a child confidence in his ability to contribute to group living, develop manual and social skills and encourage a sense of pride in his surroundings.

Unless children are very young, they should be expected to

do personal chores such as making their beds and keeping their rooms orderly and clean. They should also share responsibility for maintaining cleanliness and order in common rooms such as kitchens, bathrooms, porches, living and dining areas, as well as in the immediate grounds around their cottage. These tasks convey a sense of obligation and contribution to their "home," which in any wholesome family is a collective responsibility of parents and children. Unless their child care workers convey a sense of dedication to maintaining attractive living space, the children cannot be expected to approach their tasks enthusiastically. Whenever possible, children should participate in planning work assignments, and evaluation of the group's success in carrying out its responsibilities for cottage maintenance should take place at the weekly cottage meeting. Supervising workers should be available to help those who require assistance during clean-ups and should offer objective criticism, including approval, for jobs well done.

Children may be constructively involved in beautifying their surroundings. Enthusiasm can be evoked for decorating bedrooms, common rooms and cottage grounds when staff and children plan and work together. Adult guidance and supervision are essential because children in residence may be unrealistic in their initial conception of a project, of the work involved and of the materials they request.

For example, boys in one adolescent cottage decided to paint their rooms. No one told them there were unacceptable colors. Several of the boys wanted to paint their rooms in "way-out" colors such as deep red or dark brown, and were angry when their choice was disapproved. One boy defiantly painted his ceiling and walls a deep brown one night. Similarly, a girl, who was deeply depressed following her father's death and had suicidal thoughts, painted her room and her bed black. Symbolically, she had converted her room into a tomb. In both cases pathogenic factors rather than esthetic considerations determined the selection of colors. Depressing surroundings were not good for these children and the rooms had to be repainted.

If a project is not geared to the children's capacities and available resources, the children's initial enthusiasm may wane quickly. In addition to guidance in planning, they will need support, help and supervision in completing it.

The value of work and respect for it can be conveyed to children if adults demonstrate concretely through actual participation. A worker who asks children to do work which he himself will not do is doing a disservice to the concept of the positive value of work. Indirectly, he conveys the attitude that work is something to be avoided or to be imposed on others. A child care worker who rationalizes his demands on children to clean their rooms or do assigned house chores on the basis that this is required by "administration" conveys a negative attitude about work as an essential in group living and influences children to view work as an imposed burden. The worker who demands order and cleanliness in children's rooms while his own is messy is neither respected nor readily obeyed.

Worker's Observations

The Group

1. Are the children involved in planning for household tasks, rotation schedules and distribution of work assignments? Or is this achieved by posting designated assignments without involving the children?
2. Are the children involved in evaluating their performances in household tasks through weekly cottage group meetings?
3. Do the children care about the appearance of their rooms or common living areas?
4. Are they cooperative in carrying out such tasks?

5. What are the disruptive elements that prevent a sense of group cohesiveness around the physical appearance of the cottage?
6. Are there any particular children whom you resent because of their negative attitude toward work?

The Individual Child

1. Does he enjoy doing the work assigned? Does he carry it out responsibly?
2. Does he passively accept a work assignment without motivation to carry it out?
3. Does he resist doing assigned chores?
4. While working, does he easily get discouraged, frustrated, or angry?
5. Does he seek help from the child care worker?
6. Does he learn a task easily?
7. Does he ask for approval?
8. Does he rationalize mistakes?
9. Does he blame others for his failings?

Self-Awareness Questions

1. Do you believe in the value of the work you ask the children to perform?
2. Do you feel that too much work is expected of the children? Is too little expected?
3. Do you like working with them or do you limit your role to supervising and checking whether the work is done?
4. Do you convey respect for the value of work orderliness and cleanliness through action rather than words?
5. Do you prefer assigning chores and work projects to involving the children in discussion about planning, execution, and evaluation of achievement?

CLOTHING AND GROOMING

Clothing has social and emotional connotations in addition to its practical functions of protecting the body. The former takes on greater significance as the child gets older. Clothing that is drab, worn out, shabby and dirty does not necessarily represent economic poverty. To a child, it may signify lack of concern and care on the part of adults and it contributes to a sense of feeling inadequate, worthless and rejected.

Children in residence reflect prevailing peer attitudes regarding clothing and this may become an arena of conflict between children and child care workers. Even young children want to be dressed in the current style, a need which becomes even more important among preadolescents and young teenagers. Nuances of individuality seem to become more important in later adolescence. Child care workers have to be sensitive to children's attitudes and preferences regarding style of dress; however, they should not condone extreme fads in clothing which are socially unacceptable, contrary to the rules established by the institution or excessively expensive.

Child care workers can help in the selection of appropriate clothing and in its maintenance. Children usually need to be reminded to lay out clothes before bedtime so that they will be easily available the next morning. They need to be taught proper attitudes and skills to keep clothes clean, directed to wear appropriate protection against rain and snow, and have their clothing checked for repair and replacement. The child care worker frequently accompanies children on shopping trips and helps them select the best available quality at the most economical price. Relationships with children can be enhanced by the interest expressed in their appearance.

The following excerpt from an institution's policy on clothing illustrates the significance of the child care worker's role:

The manner in which clothing is provided has implications far beyond that of merely keeping the children adequately clothed. For example, the concern we have in seeing our children adequately clothed, the pains we take in developing in our children a feeling of pride and dignity in their appearance is the real substance which makes for relationship between a child care worker and child. Too, there is real educational value in helping our children shop for clothing, realize what clothing costs, and appreciate the responsibilities of taking care of their belongings. . . . From the day of admission on, the child care worker will have the major responsibility for the child's clothing, its upkeep, repair, and replacement, in accordance with the demands of the basic wardrobe . . . [A list of basic clothing is given, with suggestions regarding appropriate kind of dress for school, play and weekends.]

All items of clothing belonging to a child are clearly marked with the child's name. This has value for recovering clothing items which may be misplaced or get mixed among another child's clothing. It also has value in giving the child a feeling of individual possession and can foster a sense of responsibility in the child with respect to his clothing. From time to time it becomes necessary to check through the children's clothing for marking, since with wear and cleaning, the names can rub out, and of course, all new items of clothing should be marked immediately. . . .

When a replacement is necessary the child care worker may arrange a shopping trip. The purpose of shopping trips with the children is to give them experience in using stores, making selections of merchandise, and gaining some appreciation of the cost of clothing. The child care worker is responsible that the clothing purchased be in good taste, appropriate to the particular child, and of good fit. Therefore, a shopping group should be small enough to be easily manageable so that the child care worker is able to give the necessary time and attention to each child.

Factors not directly related to clothing, such as child's feeling of deprivation, neglect, difference from others, need to be considered in planning purchases, but they have to be related to the reality of the institution's clothing policy. . . .

Child care workers should train girls to meet their responsibilities for taking care of their clothing. This should include washing, mending, adjusting hems, ironing, and using the washing machines. Girls should learn how to use a needle and thread, as well as matching the color of the thread with the garment. They should be able to sew buttons on their garments, repair buttonholes, and mend any garments that need repairing. This training is of real educational value in helping our girls to maintain self-respect, and developing a sense of pride and dignity in their daily appearance. Certainly, all of them, if they are to live in the community, will have to be able to do such things in order to maintain themselves properly.

About one week before the date of discharge of a child, the child care worker will go over the child's complete wardrobe with the child present and participating. The child care worker will especially check to see that all clothing presented by the child is in fact his and not another child's. The child should leave with sufficient clothing. If necessary, additional purchases should be made (Edenwald School Manual of Policies and Procedures, 1974).

Like clothing, personal hygiene and grooming represent a person's self-image. Children need adult guidance to develop and maintain good standards of caring for their bodies. Younger children may need direction and help in developing skills and establishing habits of cleanliness and grooming, such as washing, bathing, brushing teeth, care of hair and nails. The child care worker provides reminders for those children who need them constantly, supports others in their efforts to establish good grooming habits, and expresses approval for those who demonstrate satisfactory performance.

SPENDING MONEY

Child care workers have the responsibility for budgeting children's spending money. The amounts may be small but the burdens and emotional strains are great. Money, like food, has symbolic connotations, generates strong emotions and creates tensions in cottage living, just as it does in families.

All children receive spending money. Older children who depend wholly on the relatively modest monthly allowance given by an institution may find it insufficient. Some who spend it before the end of the month complain, resent those who have money, and frequently ask their child care workers for advances on next month's allowance or on fantasized sums which they may receive from home. Denial is difficult and not infrequently child care workers subsidize children from their own earnings because they cannot bear to see a child without a longed-for candy bar or ice cream, or doing without "extras" on a cottage trip, while others have more than enough. Child care workers have tried to cope with such situations by interesting the children in establishing a common cottage fund derived from sale of cottage produced crafts, or other money raising efforts. In some institutions where a child cannot keep more than a token amount, violations have been dealt with by confiscating the excess for inclusion in common funds.

Problems are created when parents during visits give spending money to children rather than to the child care workers, when they send it in letters or give it to children during home visits. Such situations must be handled expeditiously with the parents by caseworkers or during visiting time by child care workers. Clarification and explanation of the rationale for the regulations suffice for most, but not for all. Those who feel antagonistic to the institution or excessively guilty for placing a child may continue to give money surreptitiously in excess of suggested amounts to compensate for guilt feelings. Other parents cannot cope with their children's pressure or manipulations and give in to demands for money.

Children may use their money to compensate for insecurities. They may purchase luxury items which they flaunt before the others, buy excessive amounts of sweets or use money to "buy" friendships. They may tempt others to steal their money and them complain about the theft.

In a group where there is a wide range in spending money among the children, it is possible, but not always convincing, to try to convey the reality of economics to "have nots." Children from impoverished slum families may be able to understand intellectually that some children have more to spend because their parents are able to provide it, but few can accept it. They feel that they are treated unfairly; some view it as rejection by their parents; all resent the inequity between their poverty and their more affluent peers. Child care workers cannot do much about this except to appeal to administration for higher spending money standards and to try innovative methods to enrich the common fund.

When money is stolen within the cottage or used for destructive purposes such as financing runaways or purchase of alcohol or drugs, disciplinary problems arise which have to be dealt with appropriately. Caseworkers and administrative persons have to be involved. The acts as well as the consequences create strains and instabilities in group living. Action against the offenders is necessary. Cottage meetings to discus issues which interfere with harmonious group life are advisable.

CHILDREN'S MAIL

Mail from home or from friends is important. It symbolizes continued interest on the part of family and peers and a sense of caring by others. Mail should be distributed to the children as soon as it is received. Usually, child care workers pick up the mail after the children go off to school and distribute it when they meet again. In general, mail is not and should not be opened and read before delivery to the child. There may be exceptions. For example, if child care workers or caseworkers observe a markedly disturbed reaction by a child after receipt of a letter, the matter should be discussed with the child. If there is conviction that mail from certain sources is damaging to him, a clinical and administrative decision can be made to open his mail before delivery. Evidence that unauthorized money is being sent in letters should be discussed with the child as well as the parents. If it continues, then letters may be opened to confiscate the unauthorized money.

Children should not be forced to write letters home. When parents express anxiety about lack of mail, the matter should be discussed with the child. At the recommendation of a caseworker, a child care worker may ask a child whether he has written home, but at no time should he pressure him to do so. It may be advisable to designate a time during the week for letter writing; this may serve to remind children who are careless about correspondence to communicate with their families.

PLAY AND RECREATION

Play, individually or in groups, organized or unplanned, is a universal phenomenon in human life. For children it provides outlets for physical energy, emotional expression and fantasy. It provides opportunities for education, skills, incorporation of values and socialization.

Disturbed Children's Use of Play

Disturbed children, whether they are withdrawn or hyperactive, anxious or apathetic, may not feel the exuberance, joy and fun generally experienced by children during play. The withdrawn child may find greater security in individualized play which seems to provide a refuge from group living requirements. The hyperactive child, motivated by anxiety to dominate or win, deprives himself of experiencing a sense of pleasure and relaxation. For the aggressive child, play may serve as an outlet for aggressive or hostile feelings.

Since disturbed children generally do not know how to plan or utilize free time constructively, adult planning and involvement in their play and recreation are essential. In one sense, play can be viewed as authorized regression to more immature behavior. It provides a stage upon which children are permitted to enact impulses which are otherwise unacceptable. Verbalizations and actions which cannot be permitted in everyday living are acceptable when expressed in play. For children whose personality is restrictive or immature, it is important to make available certain periods in which they can relax their controls in play situations.

Planned recreation provides an opportunity in which a child can relax, can reorganize his ego strengths, and then return to the more serious business of the day's activities. A recreational program should provide different types of activities or forms of play adapted to meet the therapeutic needs of different kinds of children. For example, a hostile, aggressive child in a group game such as baseball or basketball will tend to make it an intense rivalry situation. Because of group disapproval or other sanctions employed against any of his efforts to disrupt the game, he will begin to see the usefulness of rules and required behavior in group play. This provides education in cooperative activity. A youngster who is inhibited can be helped to use play to drain off a great deal of repressed hostility which may immobilize him. Participation in group games regulated to his capacity may gradually help him express suppressed aggressive impulses in constructive ways, and at the same time serve as a socializing experience.

The child care worker involved in play with children, whether it is in the cottage activities or in the formal recreation program, has opportunities to teach skills, rules of games, and sportsmanship, and, through active participation, strengthen his relationship with children. His observations have significance for diagnostic evaluation and treatment planning, and these should be shared with his co-workers during appropriate conferences.

Whereas most younger children can be interested in organized recreational activities available in the institution or in off-ground trips and sporting, cultural or entertainment events, many adolescents will resist becoming involved, preferring to be left alone to do as they wish. This laissez-faire attitude generally ends up in television viewing, hanging around, often listlessly, and frequent complaints of being bored because there is "nothing to do." It is not suprising that child care workers get discouraged by lack of responsiveness to their efforts to interest the residents in recreational activities, or at times angry as a result of hours wasted in isolation or in unjustified griping.

Nevertheless, negativism, lethargy and apathy may be manifestations of the youngsters' emotional difficulties rather than attempts to frustrate their workers. To counteract this behavior, discussion is suggested, individually and in groups, about the reasons for it. Forced participation is generally ineffective and counterproductive. Encouragement of planned activities may counteract the anxiety and lethargy present in many adolescents. This seems a constructive alternative which is within the scope and responsibility of the therapeutic milieu.

Leisure Time Cottage Activities

Even in large institutions, where recreation is centralized through a recreation department and takes place outside of the cottage living situation, there are free hours within the cottage which can be used constructively and enjoyably in activities programmed by child care workers. A supply of materials and skill training are prerequisites which must be provided by the institution. The worker's interest and investment in planning and participation with the children are crucial. According to Whittaker (1969, pp. 103-112), the worker's enthusiasm and enjoyment in a creative activity, game or sports "provide a model for the children of how a person relates to an activity." Before deciding on a particular activity, a number of variables should be considered. These include skill competency of staff, availability of the necessary materials and tools, sufficiency of staff coverage, the children's interest and motivation, and the particular mood of the group. The nature and timing of the event are also important. Thus, physically active and stimulating games should be avoided prior to bedtime; quiet games, group singing or story telling for younger children are preferable. A diversity of activities, including imaginative innovations in the rules of established games, may stimulate children's interest and enthusiasm. Flexibility in switching from one activity to another is advisable if the one that had been planned does not seem to evoke a positive response from the children.

A comprehensive cottage activity program contributes to individual and group development. It includes arts and crafts, group games and sports, creative work projects, dramatics and music, nature walks, and camping.

Arts and crafts offer a diversity of interesting and meaningful opportunities for developing skills in working with materials, creating outlets for excess energy, and deriving satisfaction from completing a creative task. Abundance of materials is essential. These need not be expensive. Newsprint and scrap materials, such as cloth remnants, plastic or wood, can be used imaginatively in such activities. Drawing, painting, and clay modeling are particularly appropriate for individual children who are reluctant or not quite ready for sports or group games.

They provide constructive outlets for frustration, draining off tension and anxiety. Some children may be fearful about using certain materials or tools and will require guidance, skill training and encouragement. Others, who get discouraged easily, lose interest and want to terminate a project which they started, will require adult support to continue working. The child who is restless and impatient, should be started off with a simple type of activity which he can complete rather quickly, and which does not require too much concentration. Success in the simpler tasks may give this child a degree of confidence to try more complex activities.

Games and sports promote social interaction, an experience in cooperation, an education in following the rules of the games, and an outlet for physical energy. Some groups may need more supervision and structure than others. Emphasis on enjoyment rather than on competitiveness, the process of the game rather than winning, should be encouraged. Children who are anxious and insecure in group activities may lack skill or confidence and will shy away from participating, while the aggressive, power-driven youngster may exploit others in activities focused on competition. The attitude of staff in encouraging enjoyment rather than competition may contribute to an atmosphere of cooperation and sharing in the joy of play, rather than one of strife.

Musical activities ranging from listening to records together, to group singing, musical games and rhythm bands also provide group participation and enjoyment. Puppetry and dramatic performances require more preparation and are excellent outlets for individual talent, for team work, and satisfaction for both performers and spectators.

There are activities which can be planned for leisure hours which not only provide recreation, but also contribute constructive work projects within the children's living space. These would include decorating individual rooms, common rooms, and the outside of the cottage, including gardening or construction of game or play areas. These offer extensive opportunities for joint planning between children and staff, skill development, cooperative work, esthetic development and a sense of achievement in beautifying one's surroundings.

Finally, there are outdoor activities like walks, hikes and camping which expand children's perceptions and experience about nature. Special consideration must be given to children's fears and anxieties evoked by overnight camping. Sufficient staff must be available for coverage in emergencies.

The camping trip, the dramatic performance or the joint cottage project culminates in enjoyment for the children. The process of planning and carrying out these activities contributes to socialization and individual growth. For example, in one residential setting, a cottage of young children and their child care workers have had a tradition of planning a two-week camping trip during the summer. They work all year on projects to finance it. They have made arts and crafts objects for a "cottage fair," had lunches and parties which earned them money to buy camping equipment and supplies. Parents have also become involved and the institution has matched the children's earnings. It has been an exciting, constructive experience for all, especially the children who felt that their effort and labor made the summer camping trip possible.

Television

Television viewing is an important leisure time activity in our society for children as well as adults. Unfortunately it can be misused. It becomes an obstacle to relationships when it is used as a substitute for personal interaction. When children are indiscriminantly exposed to inappropriate, frightening programs and films of violence, it is harmful.

Its use in residential living to fill empty leisure hours is evidently poor planning of cottage activities. A television set kept running throughout the day and evening, serving as a shelter for children who cluster around it for hours on end, is an example of adult thoughtlessness. Unplanned and unstructured television viewing can be destructive because children will frequently select programs which stir up anxiety. Younger children, exposed to horror films—especially before bedtime—may have difficulty falling asleep and may have frightening dreams or nightmares. Further, it may serve to reinforce aggressive tendencies in older children.

Children who are highly suggestible and have poor impulse control, as well as poor reality judgment, may reenact destructive scenes viewed on television. For example, this occurred in a girls' cottage. The girls had asked the child care workers for permission to view the film *Born Innocent* which portrayed some gruesome scenes, insensitive staff attitudes, a rioting group of girls in a girls' institution. The following night two of the girls organized a renactment of the riot scene and influenced most of the other girls to join them. Though some of the girls had questions about it, they followed the delinquent leaders' request because they were afraid of retaliation against them. During the disturbance, they messed up the cottage but did not physically hurt the child care workers. Intervention by administrative staff stopped the rioting and restablished controls. The girls spent hours clearing up the mess and the leaders were disciplined. During subsequent discussion with staff as well as the girls, it became clear that it was an error to let the girls view this film.

Staff control of television viewing is important because it minimizes the risks enumerated above, and because it ensures appropriate use of a potentially educational and therapeutic instrument. Through familiarity with television programming, a child care worker can plan constructive use of television viewing. The weekly *TV Guide* should enable a worker to determine which programs are appropriate for his group and which should be avoided. Children can be involved in selecting programs for those deemed acceptable by the cottage staff. If a child or a group desires to see programs of sadism and violence, the request should not be granted. However, reasons for the refusal should be stated clearly.

Staff participation in viewing television with the children can be constructive. It represents participating and sharing time together; it also provides opportunities to talk with the children about the content of a program afterwards. The discussion may be educational in nature or reassuring if some of the scenes were frightening. Even a film like *Born Innocent*, which in the case described above stimulated destructive acting-out, could have been utilized for constructive purposes if the staff had been ready to talk about the film after it was over. The anxieties and negative feelings stimulated could have been exposed, feelings and attitudes about institutional living and what it means to the children in the group might have been expressed and comparisons between cottage living in the film and in the girls' cottage could then have been made.

The worker cannot be the guardian of the television at all times. There are occasions when he may be the only child care worker on duty, or he may be busy with a problem situation, or preparing snacks, etc. At such times he may have to depend on the television set to occupy the children. There is nothing wrong with this, but the children should be told that they are being left on their own and that the worker expects them to behave. Whenever possible, the worker should make a periodic check to insure that everything is going well.

(For more detailed activity programming by child care workers, the following references are suggested: Chapter 12, "Developmental Programming for the Worker" and its Appendix, pp. 203-257 in Foster Vanderven et al., *Child Care Work with Emotionally Disturbed Children*, Pittsburgh, University of Pittsburgh Press, 1972, and "Program Activities, Their Selection and Use in a Therapeutic Milieu" by James K. Whittaker, in *The Other 23 Hours,* A. E. Treischman et al., Chicago, Aldine Publishing Co. 1969, pp. 100-119.)

Volunteers

Volunteers serve in residential treatment in a number of capacities, including teacher assistants, tutors, recreation specialists or aides, and companions to children. The volunteer "is an adult who stands somewhere between a parent person and a peer and represents a bridge between adult and peer relationships" (Hirschfield and Starr, 1971, p. 98).

In terms of leisure-time activities, the volunteer assigned to a child provides essential relationships and social activities on grounds or outside the institution on a regular continuing basis. In the case of "Big Brothers" and "Big Sisters" the child has opportunities to spend time in their homes, which by selection represent harmonious family living.

Child care workers are (or should be) consulted about the assignment of a child to a volunteer. Knowing their children intimately, they can be helpful in the selection of one appropriate to a particular child's personality and needs, as well as his readiness to participate in a relationship with a friendly, interested adult other than his relatives or staff. The relationship between volunteer and child care worker is friendly and non-competitive. It is generally not as intensive or as extensive as that between the volunteer and the child's caseworker, who generally supervises the volunteer's activities. The volunteer should be given recognition for his contribution to a child's treatment and the child care workers can, by their attitude, convey appreciation when the volunteer visits the cottage.

Observations of Play Activities

Individual Child

1. Does he prefer individual play or group activities?
2. Is his play reality oriented or primarily "make-believe" or fantasy? If predominantly "make-believe," does he switch back to reality quickly? Does he do so reluctantly or with difficulty?
3. What kind of group activities does he prefer?
   a. Active or passive games?
   b. Competitive or non-competitive?
   c. Athletic or esthetic, such as dance, music?
   d. Does he prefer watching TV to games?
4. Does he have any special interests or hobbies?
5. Does he have any special skills or talents? Is he eager to learn new skills or is he fearful or evasive?
6. Is he a leader or a follower in games?
7. Is he:
   > well coordinated?
   > poorly coordinated or clumsy?
   > inhibited?
   > spontaneous?
8. Is he destructive with toys or equipment?
9. Does he:
   > conform to the rules of a game?
   > try to dominate a group activity?
   > cheat or try to, in order to win?
   > try to avoid getting into group play?
   > blame others if the team loses?

   Is he:
   > aggressive, even hurting playmates?
   > disruptive in a game?
10. Does he have "fun," enjoy himself at play?
11. Is he fearful of getting hurt?

12. Is he reckless, accident prone?
13. Is he accepted and liked by his playmates?
14. What is his attitude toward recreation staff? Is he friendly, hostile, ambivalent or indifferent?

The Group

1. Is it easy or difficult for the group as a whole to get involved in group activities?
2. Are there subgroups (two or three children) who enjoy playing together?
3. Is the group responsive to planned activities?
4. What kind of activities or group games do they prefer?
5. Is it easy or difficult to get them involved in planning group activities?
6. Are they responsive to worker's suggestions?
7. Can they function as a "team," a cohesive group?
8. Does the group have a "natural" leader?
9. Are there isolates who do not get involved in group activities?
10. Is anyone treated as a "scapegoat" by the others?

The Worker

1. Do you enjoy organizing play activities?
2. Do you feel insecure about organizing group activities?
3. Do you like to play with a child individually, with small groups, or with the total group?

BEDTIME

Just as waking poses anticipated difficulties for some children, bedtime evokes anxieties because sleep implies uncertainties, helplessness and loss of control. Some children are fearful of potential nightmares; a few may be afraid that, once asleep, they may not awaken the next day; others may perceive sleep as a threat because they will not be in control of what goes on about them while they are asleep.

Fear of falling asleep was dramatically exemplified by 10-year-old Marcia who, after admission to the residential treatment center, would cry and complain she could not fall asleep unless the child care worker on duty was near her bedside. It was not certain at first that this might be related to the fact that Marcia's twin sister (who had been ill with leukemia for a number of years) had died in her sleep. Nightly, the worker reassured Marcia that she would watch over her while she was asleep. Subsequently, Marcia told the worker that she had been afraid to fall asleep because she believed that, like her sister, she would die in her sleep. Reassurance by both child care workers and Marcia's therapist that she was physically well, that no one would hurt her while she was asleep, and that she would awaken each morning finally dispelled the child's anxiety. She could then fall asleep without the physical presence of an adult guardian whom she trusted.

Anxiety Manifestations

Most young children require adult reassurance that they will be safe when asleep. For some, to be tucked in by their worker conveys that the adult cares and will protect them. A warm "good night" is reassuring. A child anxious about going to sleep will generally express it in behavior which conveys stress. He may stall, cry, demand a drink of water or go to the bathroom frequently. To postpone going to bed he may insist on watching television or he may get himself involved in play. Some children may even start fights; others may try to monopolize the worker's attention either by clinging or by provocative behavior; some are afraid of the dark, others will anticipate "bad" dreams; some will go through a number of compulsive rituals such as excessive washing or arranging items of clothing in a particular way.

Children's Objections

Some young children, especially those who had no regular bedtime hours at home, resist going to bed because they are used to staying up late, playing or watching television. This may be understandable but the worker cannot compromise the regularly set bedtime hours. Actually, the time set for young children's bedtime is not unreasonable and this should be explained to them. Occasionally, exceptions may be made by staff when there are special community events or educational television programs which would be of benefit to the children.

There are realistic difficulties with bedtime hours for adolescents. This is especially true in relation to the economics of staff time rather than children's needs. If work schedules end at 9:30 P.M. or even 10:00 P.M. there may be validity in complaints by the children that bedtime is too early, especially on weekends.

During many years of the author's experience in a residential treatment unit for emotionally disturbed adolescent boys, there were interminable arguments against a 9:30 P.M. bedtime. We could not say "You are growing, active boys and need more rest." To do so would have been hypocritical. The honest explanation about staff scheduling seemed more acceptable to the boys. This unrealistic bedtime also nourished an underground night life of disruptive behavior. Eventually, bedtime was extended to 10:30 P.M.—later for weekend activities.

Preparation

Advance planning is necessary to create a peaceful, calm atmosphere for the group in general. The involvement of staff in activities preparatory to bedtime contributes to reduction of tensions as well as to a greater closeness among children and adults. Among these are reminding the children in advance to terminate play and television watching, supervision of showering, putting out clothes for the following day, talking together. Tucking in the younger children, reading or telling a bedtime story, and reassurance that one will see them the following morning are helpful. If there is a policy or established routine that after lights are out there is to be no running, playing radios or loud conversation, it should be enforced. It is advisable for workers to perform bed-checks.

Adequate night coverage by administrative personnel and infirmary staff, as well as by child care workers, is essential for security and safety. This serves to deter acting-out among older children—inter-cottage visiting, especially in co-ed settings, runaways, kangaroo courts, abuse of individual children, and vandalism. Night staff should be especially informed regarding any special difficulty an individual child or group has experienced during the day, and any problems that are anticipated.

Because going to sleep is not easy for children who are emotionally distressed, sending a child early to bed as punishment is at best a questionable procedure. According to Gardner (1973, p. 185) it is not appropriate to associate sleep with punishment. Firstly, it is ineffective because one can send a child early to bed but not to sleep; secondly, it is destructive because using early-to-bed as a punishment reinforces the notion that there is indeed something bad about getting to sleep. Use of early bedtime as a disciplinary measure, especially for young children, is risky. Sleep problems may develop as a consequence.

Observations of Bedtime Behavior

Individual Child

    1. Are there any problems about getting him to bed? Does he dawdle, object to getting ready, become

disruptive, start arguments, try to manipulate the
worker into letting him stay up?
2. Does he express anxiety about anticipated nightmares, or that he might be hurt while asleep, or fear
that he might not awaken the following morning?
3. Is he enuretic and, if so, does he express anxiety
about it?
4. Does he masturbate after going to bed?
5. Once asleep, does he sleep through the night, or is
there restlessness, talking in his sleep, walking in his
sleep, or frequent awakening to go to the bathroom?

DISCIPLINE AND PUNISHMENT

Discipline and punishment are interrelated but not synony-
mous. Discipline may be broadly defined as the degree of established order to facilitate group living. Punishment is "a
planful attempt by adults to influence either the behavior or
the long-range development of a child, or a group of children,
for its own benefit, by exposing it to an unpleasant experience" (Redl, 1966, p. 363). "Punishment emphasizes pen-
alty. . . . Discipline, on the other hand, emphasizes the educative value of the disciplinary measure to the wrongdoer"
(Gardner, 1973, p. 163).

A therapeutic milieu depends primarily on relationships
between the children and staff to ensure conformity to the
regulations of the general structure and the rules of cottage
living in particular. Violations should first be dealt with by
individual or group discussions to educate the children about
the necessity to comply with requirements of structure. Offenders should be forewarned regarding the consequences of repeated violations. Actual punishment or deprivation is the final
step or action taken by a child care worker to convey to children the seriousness of wrongdoing.

Punishment

There is a parallel between punishment and frustration. Frustration is a universal human experience and, in tolerable doses, essential for healthy and mature development. Disciplinary measures, not unlike frustration, can be constructive if they are consistently imposed, do not exceed the frustration tolerance of a particular child, are not arbitrarily imposed at the whim or impulse of the adult, and are not accompanied by hostility or motivated by a sense of revenge.

In group living situations, punishment is generally instituted following repeated breaches of established rules. It is essential that rules be clearly stated so that both children and adults understand them. To avoid confusion among the children and conflict among the staff, these must be consistently enforced by all the workers involved with a particular group of children. Reminding a child about violations of expectations is generally advisable and should precede punishment. The actual mode of punishment may involve suspension of privileges, extra work assignments, restriction to the cottage or to one's room and other types of deprivation.

Avoiding Power Struggles

Power struggles may result in an impasse and consequent misuse of punishment. With seriously disturbed children a power struggle may lead to such a rigidity of reaction on the part of the child that irrationality will replace any reasoning capacity the child may have when not under severe stress. It may even lead to uncontrollable temper tantrums. In such situations, the child care worker who becomes involved in an irrational confrontation risks being the loser. The loss involves important consequences to his relationship with the child and his status in the group. The other children may lose respect for the worker's authority. Some of them may become anxious because the sense of security that adult authority provides has been shaken by their perception of the worker's loss of control. Diamond (1973) offers the following commendable suggestions to his new child care workers:

1. Don't become involved in any confrontation unless you are sure you can win.
2. Don't make threats you will not follow through.
3. Don't make threats you cannot follow through.

A worker who does not follow this advice may tempt the children to test his firmness and strength and to undermine his authority. In general a new worker should avoid responsibility for meting out punishment or restrictions until he is fully familiar with the children and the expectations of the institution. During this period, consultation with fellow workers and supervisors can be most helpful.

Preventive Intervention

Actual punishment may at times be avoided by preventive intervention. A child care worker may interfere in a volatile argument between children before it reaches an explosive level or physical assault. He may initiate group discussion about irritating situations which contribute to the group's acting-out in destructive ways. If a worker becomes aware of a potential delinquent act by an individual or group, he should intervene by bringing the issues into open discussion. He should be willing and ready to state categorically to a potential runaway: "I am not going to let you do it, I will not stand by and let you hurt yourself." Or, "I am not going to let you hurt him." Or, "I am not going to let you destroy that."

If a child seems to be working himself into an uncontrollable outburst which might result in injury to himself or to others, he may have to be isolated from the group for a brief period, preferably in the cottage. However, if a child behaves in a seriously unstable manner and the worker's efforts to stabilize him are unsuccessful, recommendations should be made to the superior or administrator on duty to transfer the child out of the cottage to an "isolation" room in the infirmary, if such is available, or to a similar facility where he would be under adult supervision and observation and where he would also have an opportunity to talk to his caseworker or psychiatrist, as needed. This often helps a child over a serious emotional crisis and avoids the need to transfer him temporarily to a psychiatric hospital.

Punishment Criteria

Before deciding on a specific punishment, the worker should consider whether it will help the child to learn not to repeat the offense. If it will not be effective, then it is improper. If a particular punishment is destructive to the relationship between the child and the worker, an alternative should be chosen. Other considerations include:

1. Punishment should be administered as soon after the offensive behavior as possible. Delay may cause the child to forget what he did to deserve it. He will not connect his responsibility to the consequences and will project blame on the worker, considering him unfair.

2. Excessive punishment is unfair as well as abusive. The child will focus on the unfairness of the adult, rather than his own responsibility.

3. The disciplinary act should not be motivated by hostility. If it is, the child senses the hostility and views the punishment as vengeance rather than justice.

Some offenses may be neurotically motivated. For example, stealing or lying (elaborated in a later section, see p.   ) may be an expression of neurotic conflict or neurotic needs. It is unlikely that punishment will help to stop this behavior. In such cases, the worker should involve the child's therapist or caseworker to deal with this symptomatic behavior. In contrast, there are children who lie or steal because they do not consider it wrong. This may be a consequence of identification with established values in their families or neighborhoods. These children view punishment for such offenses as unjust. Here, punishment does not suffice. A more appropriate approach is to focus on reeducation from delinquent to ethically and morally acceptable values. This takes time and will be accomplished only when these children form identifications with significant adults who represent socially acceptable values.

The nature of the child's personality, his cultural background and the degree of his pathology need to be considered. The caseworker or therapist can help the child care worker to differentiate between the significance of disciplinary action or punishment to a sociopathic youngster who strives to avoid it, its meaning to a neurotic child who wants to be punished in order to have neurotic guilt alleviated, and its connotation to a provocative masochistic individual who wants punishment because he experiences it as pleasure.

Group Punishment

As a rule, group punishment should be avoided. Redl (1966, p. 359) states: "An intervention technique . . . should at least be 'harmless' in terms of its effects on the group, or at worst, it should not produce more negative group effects than we can handle." Group punishment is especially inappropriate as a means of forcing a group of children to expose an unknown culprit. The concept is contrary to the adolescent group code and is perceived as "blackmail" to force them to turn against a peer. Even if the use of "strong arm methods" or threats of severe punishment is successful, the price the adult pays in resentment, hostile feelings, and loss of respect more than counteracts the gains or adult "victory." It may be more advisable to convene a group meeting to discuss the issues and to encourage expression of opinion or decision by the group, a procedure that frequently results in identification of the wrongdoer by voluntary confession. Of course, there is one situation when this method may result in injustice: In a delinquent group, an innocent youngster, generally the group's scapegoat, may be forced to confess to an act he did not perform to protect someone in favored or power status position. Workers who know their groups are not easily fooled by such subterfuge.

Neither should the peer group be utilized as a jury and judge of an individual offender. Disturbed and delinquent children do not make objective juries nor benevolent judges. They can act as cruel executioners. Consequently, trial by peer courts should be outlawed rather than encouraged. Such "kangaroo courts" do not represent democratic processes nor a constructive aspect of "student government" in institutions for disturbed, delinquent children.

Physical Punishment

Physical punishment as a method of control or as a means of asserting adult authority is inhumane and for the most part does not work. According to Karl Menninger, "The sock-it-to-'em theory (punishment to deter crime) of controlling frustration and anger and greed is futile and self defeating. It isn't just unfair or unjust. It is ineffective" (Menninger, 1968). At best it may temporarily suppress an undesirable behavior or displace it. Children view physical punishment as personal attacks. For the emotionally disturbed child, it seems to be an inappropriate reinforcer of learning because it feeds his distrust of adults, hindering the development of positive relationships. The provocations constantly faced by child care workers cannot be minimized. When a worker reacts physically to extreme provocation, it is understandable because everyone's threshhold of tolerance can be breached. Children should be made aware of this. But as a prevalent technique of intervention, it is neither educational nor therapeutic. In fact, corporal punishment in children's institutions is prohibited by law in most states. In the event that a staff member is provoked to react physically, he is required to write a detailed statement regarding the incident.

The following excerpt from one institution's manual of policies and procedures, addressed to its child care staff, illustrates its firm position about corporal punishment:

> Discipline, to be effective, should be based on a healthy relationship between you and the child. A child who values your goodwill, friendship, approval and affection will be more likely to respond positively to your efforts to set limits. This will be particularly so if you make it clear to the child that you are disapproving of the child's behavior and not of the child himself.
>
> Corporal punishment of children is not only a most serious violation of this Agency's policy, but also a direct violation of the Rules of the New York State Board of Social Welfare.
>
> *Corporal punishment includes any of the following:*
>
> A. Striking a child.
> B. Shaking, shoving, pinching.
> C. Punishment by another child at the instigation of an adult.
> D. Punishment by the group at the instigation of an adult.
> E. Punishment by forcing a child to take a certain position: squatting, bending, standing against a wall.

It is sometimes necessary to restrain a child who has, for one reason or another, lost control of himself and is in danger of doing physical harm to himself, other children or a staff member. In this event, it is the obligation of the adult to use physical restraint as a preventive measure. Of course, it is a matter of judgment as to just how much physical restraint is needed in such cases. Fortunately, this is not a frequent occurrence, but when it does become necessary, staff should keep in mind the following:

A. Use only that amount of physical restraint that is actually needed to gain control of the situation.

B. If you are able to keep control of your own anger in the situation, you will be able to handle the situation more adequately.

C. Even while you are restraining the child, talk to him, try to calm him, try to communicate the idea that you want to let go as soon as he indicates that he himself has gained control. (Sometimes the mere fact that you are holding the child longer than seems necessary or with more force than is needed can result in prolonging the incident.)

D. Use physical restraint only when you are certain that you have exhausted all other means of gaining control (Edenwald School Manual of Policies and Procedures, 1974.

This type of policy, which is an outgrowth of the institution's treatment philosophy and New York State Board of Social Welfare Rules, presents a framework of expectations for its staff. It clearly defines what a child care worker cannot do to a child and suggests alternatives. Another child caring agency might phrase its policy differently but all would have to prohibit corporal punishment. Workers have been critical of the inclusion of "shaking" and "shoving" as physical punishment; others have raised issues regarding self-defense in situations of assault: "What am I supposed to do when I'm attacked?" "Should I not use physical means against a big bully who is beating up another child?" Such questions have validity and require clarification by supervisors and administrators. There must also be a firm policy regarding physical attack on staff by children. Both children and staff must be assured a sense of security from injury.

Not unlike other adults in the general population, there are child care workers who continue to believe in the platitude "Spare the rod, spoil the child." Although most child care workers are not in favor of corporal punishment as a method of control, it is not unusual to hear workers who deal with severely disturbed, impulse-ridden children and violence-prone youth express the wish that they had the option to react physically against extreme defiance and provocation. They complain that many of these children take advantage of existing policies against corporal punishment. They attack the rights of others because they know that they cannot be handled roughly. King (1976, p. 48) states, "The flaunting of rights is the single most provocative weapon that these kids use, particularly when it's coupled with an expression of guiltlessness, of open contempt for the very considerations they are being offered."

In seminar sessions conducted by the author this concern was frequently expressed. A number of very pertinent questions were raised: "Is it not better to hit a kid who drives you to desperation by his defiance, threats, negativism, or abuse of other children than to hate and reject him?" "How are these youths, who won't listen to us, to learn right from wrong?" "If talking and teaching by example do not convince a boy (or girl) that his destructive behavior is not good for him, what can we do?" Several houseparents with decades of service in child care talked with fondness about visits from their former charges who reminded them of long forgotten incidents of painful confrontation which they still considered had been most helpful to them. One man had told his cottage mother,

"I never forgot the beating you gave me—it hurt but I knew you did it because you cared. It helped to straighten me out."

The common thread weaving through all of these reminiscences was a genuine adult concern and caring for the children they had hit. This, rather than the physical act of punishment, could have been the significant factor that registered and turned out to be beneficial for the young man quoted above. It was obvious that none of these workers had enjoyed hitting children; all had felt badly afterwards; no one was sure physical punishment would have worked equally as well for other children in their care.

This led to a discussion of the danger inherent in allowing individual discretion regarding use of corporal punishment. Some expressed concern that it might be abused. Some workers might punish cruelly, to "get back" at kids who were disliked; for others it might serve as an easy way to achieve conformity and stability in a cottage group. It might be "nice" for staff but harmful to children. In view of these reservations, many of these workers expressed themselves in favor of retaining the prohibition against corporal punishment.

The child care worker's dilemma regarding management of the violence-prone youth without resorting to counter-violence may be controlled by agency policy prohibiting physical punishment. However, his conflicting feelings may persist. King suggests "the necessity for constant team cooperation, review, supervision and direction towards the objective of bringing into disciplined play the understanding of feelings in the work with these youths" (King, 1976, p. 51). He urges training in the recognition of feeling and sensitivity to the causes that generate them. In a confrontation with a defiant, aggressive youth, the worker must be ready to tell him how he feels about the provocation. If counter-violent feelings are evoked, it should be expressed but assurance given that it will not be enacted. The violence-prone youth expects counter-violence from others. He has to be convinced that those who care for him can control him without resorting to it. He has to be helped to substitute thought for impulsive action. In this way, "these youths can begin to learn to cope with the frightening violence that controls their lives by surviving new experiences in a different way, and by incorporation of the new way into their styles of life" (King, 1975, p. 143).

Role of Administrative Staff

Supervisory and administrative staff are physically at a greater social distance from the child and therefore have a lesser impact on his behavior and development than do child care workers or teachers who live and work closely with him. They are, however, important as symbols of authority to children. They play a role in establishing and maintaining the "structure" of the residential program and delegate to others enforcement of its requirements. They are rarely involved as disciplinarians. However, some situations may require direct intervention by higher administrative authority, especially in crisis situations which have an impact on the institution as a whole. Direct involvement by the chief administrator with a child or group of children is advisable in cases of individual or group vandalism, car theft, burglary or assault within or outside the boundaries of the institution. This serves a number of constructive purposes: It conveys to the offender(s) the concern of the highest level of authority for them as individuals as well as for all the children and staff of the institution; it reaffirms staff responsibility to uphold standards for the safety and protection of persons or property; and it symbolizes the help the institution is ready to extend to children in order to help them curb destructive behavior. This "talking to" needs to be supplemented with opportunities for "talking with" in order to involve children and staff in coping with crises. These discussions with children and staff may stimulate rethinking of important issues related to communal living. The interactional processes which this stimulates may contribute to a greater sense of cohesiveness and social responsibility.

Examples of crisis situations not uncommon in residential settings are offered for purposes of illustration:

1. A group of adolescent boys leave their cottage late at night and burglarize a staff apartment.
2. Youngsters from the institution get into difficulties in the neighboring community by stealing a car, burglarizing a store, or fighting with neighborhood children.
3. A group of girls run away from the institution.
4. Children returning from home visits bring in dangerous drugs for use and for distribution to other children.
5. A recently admitted boy is severely beaten by his cottage peers during initiation rites.
6. A secret kangaroo court in a cottage metes out severe physical punishment to a child.

All of the examples involve a group of children whose behavior is harmful to themselves and to others; all are destructive acts, violating institutional regulations and structure and acceptable social values; all require staff intervention. The traditional way of coping with such behavior is generally limited to disciplinary action against the offenders. This may be temporarily effective in deterring repetition of the offensive behavior. Its efficacy in effecting lasting modification of destructive attitudes and behavior is questionable.

If the goals of residential treatment are rehabilitation and (re)education in the service of mature personality development, punitive measures which at best maintain surface control over disturbed children do not suffice. Structure and behavioral standards are essential in residential treatment, and disciplinary consequences for violations of institutional requirements are in order. However, other methods of education in values are necessary supplements to disciplinary action. Residential treatment has the advantage of group living and the group processes available for therapeutic purposes. Children and staff, including the offenders, can be involved in organizing discussion groups to examine pertinent issues. The whole institution, mobilized for free interchange, of ideas, may become a symbol of common concern and mutual aid for constructive change.

Appropriate matters for group discussions in the crisis situations mentioned above might be:

Example #1, breaking into a staff apartment, represents a threat to a basic human right—a sense of personal security. Group discussion would provide an opportunity to examine causes of such behavior, its impact on children and staff, its threat to the essential atmosphere of security, the rationale for structure to curb destructive, impulsive behavior, and the need for everyone to have a sense of social responsibility and mutual aid.

Example #2 provides an opportunity to acquaint the children with the relationship of the institution to the neighboring community, the importance of maintaining a "good neighbor" policy with the people who live around them, and the consequences of destructive acts which elicit community hostility against the institution. The group could also formulate ways in which children could demonstrate to the community their regret about the harm done and plan activities for making restitution for the damage.

Discussion related to example #3 might deal with the harmful consequence of running away. This would include exposure to danger, exploitation by those who might "pick up" a girl on the road, clarification of the meaning of running away as "acting out rather than talking out" frustration, and the fact that running away disrupts the continuity of treatment.

Example #4 provides an opportunity to discuss the dangers of drug use and traffic. It might lead to development of a drug education program.

Examples #5 and #6 involve the elemental issue of physical safety and freedom from physical attack, the minimum a residential setting must guarantee to each child and member of its staff. Adult surveillance and punishment for violation of this principle are not in themselves effective deterrents to the expression of the sadism and group aggression which these examples illustrate. Both the attack on the child during initiation rites and the kangaroo court were rationalized by the children who participated in them as being socially accepted practices imitating the initiation rites practices in college fraternities and social clubs. Such rationalization does not justify the cruelty of the action, which must be prohibited formally by administration. However, to prevent such occurrences from going underground, group discussion should be initiated to help the children understand the destructive consequences to all who are involved, including judge and executioner (Adler, 1971).

SEVERE PROBLEM BEHAVIOR

Life with disturbed children in residential treatment is full of problems. The child care worker is a constant witness to, and not infrequently the object of, children's conflicts which express themselves in troubled and troubling behavior. Problem behavior encompasses a broad spectrum, ranging from withdrawal and passivity to hyperactivity, anger, hostility and aggression. It weaves through the daily routines and interaction among the children and the adults and poses difficulties for child care workers. They also have to cope with more serious problems which are very stressful. These include temper tantrums, bedwetting and soiling, lying, stealing and running away. Although administrative and clinical personnel may become involved in crises related to such behavior, their presence is not always available when needed. The child care worker may find himself very much alone, left to struggle with an extremely difficult situation and its consequences on the individual child who expresses it and the group that witnesses it.

Temper Tantrum

A temper tantrum can be as overwhelming an experience for the adult who is the object of it as it is for the child who acts it out. These tantrums are irrational, tumultuous and exhausting. The child acts as if he is oblivious to the reality of his surroundings. He may cry, scream, throw things, use abusive language, threaten assault; he may jump up and down, throw himself on the ground, thrash about, kick, pound the floor, bang his head; he may scream invectives, threats and accusations at the child care worker who is nearby, blaming him for the frustration which triggered the outburst. The child will rarely attack the adult physically. He is more likely to injure himself.

The temper tantrum is generally preceded by a phase identified by Treischman as the "rumbling and grumbling phase." Here the child seems tense and restless, exhibiting a buildup of anxiety and a deepening sense of discomfort which he tries to alleviate by seeking an issue which will provide the outlet for his accelerating inner tension. The slightest frustration can trigger the outburst. The observant worker, sensing the child's restlessness and irritation, may be able to intervene in time to prevent the temper tantrum. He may, for example, suggest to the child that something seems to be bothering him and that he would like to be helpful. If the child has had previous temper tantrums, the worker might remind him that it would be better to talk about it before the feelings build up to uncontrollable proportions which usher in a very unpleasant situation. If this is not done, or if the worker's efforts are unsuccesful, the temper tantrum will run its course (Treischman et al., 1969, p. 176).

One child care worker has described his confrontation with a child in the course of a temper tantrum as follows:

> I usually could sense when a temper tantrum was imminent for Danny when he was more than usually provocative. When I saw this sort of thing developing, I usually tried, if possible, to defuse it before it started, either by isolating him for a time or reasoning with him. If this failed, however, my first thought was always to get a physical hold on Danny. Sometimes this was necessary for purely protective reasons, for he would many times pick up weapons or throw things with anger; but I did it in any case to provide him with a physical manifestation of the control which we were providing for him. At first I merely would hold his wrists and let the screaming run its course while attempting to remain relatively passive myself. As time passed, however, I found it more efficacious to pinion him some way and let him know he would be released from the uncomfortable position as soon as he controlled himself. He was always quite provocative and abusive in a tantrum, but I always tried not to lose my temper, although I was not always successful. When the incident was over, he was repentant and quiet, and I usually would punish him in some minor way (such as staying in the cottage for a while), making the distinction to him that he was being isolated, not for being angry, but for handling his anger in a harmful and uncontrolled way (Alterman, 1973).

The child's temper tantrum represents loss of inner controls. Expression of sympathy, involvement in dialogue or negotiation to influence him to stop his irrational behavior is futile.

He does not seem to hear what is said to him. In fact, he may react more negatively and contrary to the suggestions. Threats of punishment or hurting him should also be avoided because the genuine temper tantrum is an involuntary act, the child being unconscious of the inner conflicts that produce it. He must be protected from hurting himself or others and this can be done by holding him tightly and firmly and removing him from the scene if other children are present. This avoids aggravating the intensity of the tantrum and protects the others from witnessing its course. It is not an easy task to hold a wildly thrashing, verbally abusive child. It may evoke anxiety and, not infrequently, anger in the adult. There is no harm in conveying to the child that one does not like his behavior and that it is making the worker angry. He should be told that he will not be hurt and that he will be held until he is able to reestablish controls which the worker feels he is capable of. Gradually, the irrational behavior will subside, after which the child will seem to grow limp, exhausted physically. Generally he wants to be left alone and if he requests it, his wish should be respected. He should be told, however, that the worker will be nearby and will be glad to talk to him. Some children seem to feel guilty afterwards and even apologize for the trouble they have caused. Others may act as if the temper tantrum had never occurred. As soon as the child is sufficiently recovered, it is advisable to talk over with him the events leading up to the temper tantrum. He may be asked to try to remember what made him feel so tense and to describe the feelings that preceded the outburst. One could suggest to him alternative ways to handle his feelings, such as talking things over with the worker. He should be encouraged to ask for help in the future before he "blows his top." The event should also be reported to the child's caseworker and the child should be encouraged to discuss it in his individual therapy sessions.

In the case of Danny, described above, there may have been

a connection between the temper tantrums and the boy's relationship with his disturbed, inconsistent and sexually seductive mother. It may have symbolized the sado-masochistic relationship between the two. Alterman explains:

> Danny will have engineered, out of anger, some situation in which he has been frustrated or in which he has provoked someone—an adult or another child—usually into striking him. Apparently as soon as he is struck (or some other physical contact is made), he begins to scream very loudly in the vilest obscenities possible. I have noticed that these obscenities usually refer to mothers, a fact which undoubtedly has some significance. At this point, a staff member usually has to remove him from the premises physically since he will continue to scream at the cause of his anger and struggle.
>
> I see these explosions as a sort of culmination of most of this child's characteristics. In them, he gains attention, manipulates a reaction, and tests an adult's concern for him. He shows his extreme anger and lack of impulse control and, of course, he frequently masochistically provokes others to reject and punish him.

Some temper outbursts resemble but are not actual temper tantrums. For example, when a phobic child is exposed to the object of his fear, whether it be an animal or a frightening situation, he experiences a massive surge of anxiety which breaks down his inner controls. The resulting behavior triggered by inner panic resembles a temper tantrum. However, as soon as the phobic object is removed or as soon as the child leaves the fearful, anxiety-provoking situation (such as school, in cases of school phobia), the disturbed behavior ceases. Psychotherapeutic treatment which gets at the causal conflicts responsible for the phobia may eliminate such anxiety attacks (Freud, 1965, p. 111).

There are also staged or feigned temper tantrums. They

should be handled with firmness. A child who has been successful in getting his way through a temper tantrum may learn to use it in a manipulative way to force reluctant adults to give in to his unreasonable demands. Knowing the children, a worker will soon learn if a temper tantrum staged by one of them is genuine or faked. In the latter case, the so-called "rumbling and grumbling" phase with its intensifying state of anxiety is not in evidence. The behavior outburst may be precipitated by an adult's refusal to give in to an unreasonable demand. If the action does not stop on request, the child should be isolated. The behavior may continue, but if it is ignored and does not bring the wanted results, it will subside. The child may also be disciplined for such behavior in order to reinforce awareness that it is inappropriate and unacceptable.

What is crucial in both the actual or feigned temper tantrum is for the adult not to get frightened nor show anxiety or irrational anger. The child may have been successful in the past in getting his way primarily because the adults, generally parents, became frightened and gave in to avoid the discomfort of witnessing the tantrum or struggling with the consequences. The child has learned to exploit the adults' fears.

There are also situations where a child has learned to stage a temper tantrum in order to get attention from neglectful or disinterested parents. Apparently the only way the child can attract their attention is through the shock of a temper tantrum. He may perpetuate this behavior with child care workers until he is convinced that they are not like his parents. His tantrums may then cease because he no longer views the workers in terms of his experiences with his parents. Should the child succeed in evoking a reaction on the part of the child care worker similar to that of the parents, the temper tantrum pattern will probably be reinforced and reenacted.

Bedwetting

Enuresis, the medical term for bedwetting, is a disorder of the urinary function involving involuntary passage of urine. When it occurs during waking hours it is "diurnal enuresis" and during sleeping it is "nocturnal enuresis." Enuresis is defined "as bedwetting or clotheswetting in persons over the age of three who fail to exhibit the reflex to pass urine when the impulse is felt during waking hours, and those who do not rouse from sleep of their own accord when the process is occurring during the sleeping state" (Pierce, 1967, p. 1380).

It has been estimated that 88% of children have ceased wetting by age four and one-half, 93% by age seven and one-half, and 99% by age 17. Wetting occurs twice as frequently among boys as it does among girls. In about 10% of the known cases an organic defect may be the principal cause. Consequently, when a child has both diurnal and nocturnal enuresis, a thorough medical examination is in order to rule out organic causes. When organic factors are ruled out as the causative agents, wetting may be considered as a manifestation of emotional disturbance, developmental immaturity due to faulty or inconsistent habit training, or a combination of both. The enuretic child may use his symptoms to get attention from or express hostility toward a rejecting or neglecting parent or to perpetuate infantile dependency on a mother who may consciously or unconsciously encourage it (English and Pearson, 1945, pp. 216-219).

Treatment methods include medication like Tofranil, psychotherapy, habit training suggestions such as limitation of fluids before bedtime or interruption of sleep to go to the bathroom, behavior modification or the use of conditioning devices which awaken the child by a buzzer as soon as a drop of urine contacts a wired pad on which he sleeps.

The enuretic child bears the burden of shame. Being chided

or ridiculed for lack of control of a function over which he does not have conscious control, he begins to feel demeaned, helpless, ashamed or angry at himself or his critics. A child in residential treatment who is enuretic is at a disadvantage because this symptom is not easily concealed in group living. Adult impatience with the management problems and peer ridicule aggravate the child's feelings of insecurity. He may deny the symptom, attempt to avoid its discovery by hiding his wet underwear and linens. Shaming, scolding or punishment must be avoided. It is not only useless as a measure of control but may actually reinforce the intensity of the condition. The situation should be called to the attention of medical and clinical staff for evaluation and planning of a course of treatment to which the child care worker becomes an important contributor. He may dispense prescribed medication, limit fluid intake before bedtime, or awaken the child during the night. If at all possible, treatment should not be imposed on the child against his will but achieved with his cooperation. Patience and encouragement on the part of the child care worker are vital. If the child wets the bed during the night, he should be allowed time to shower, and to deposit the soiled linen in a special container to be sent to the laundry. If wetting occurs during waking hours, he should be asked to change his underwear. The worker should express a hope that the child will be able to achieve control as soon as possible because of the social difficulties lack of control creates between the child and his peers. Encouragement should be accompanied by an offer to help him in his efforts to overcome the condition. The slightest lessening of the frequency of wetting should be rewarded by praise or any other appropriate rewards.

Soiling

Soiling, medically known as encopresis, is considered a symptom of emotional disturbance when organic causes have been ruled out by medical examination. It is not uncommon among preschool children following toilet training. "Accidents" may occur during periods of excitement or stress. The older the child, the more serious is the problem and its solution. Soiling may represent a reaction to strict and rigid toilet training, a fear reaction against a punitive parent, defiance or rebellion against rigid parental authority. Shaming, blaming or punishment is not helpful. It may, in fact, serve to aggravate the condition and add additional conflictual problems.

Soiling makes group living difficult for the child himself, his peer group, and his child care workers. The child who suffers from encopresis is an unhappy child who has experienced shaming, rejection and ridicule. He tries to hide the evidence but is unsuccessful because of the smell. He may stuff soiled underwear down the toilet causing overflows or he may hide soiled underpants in drawers or "secret" hiding places. He triggers child and adult impatience and anger and as a consequence of his condition may become the group scapegoat.

Once a plan of treatment is formulated, the child should be encouraged to follow it. He is expected to shower after a soiling incident, to go to the toilet more frequently, to change his underwear, to rinse the soiled underwear and to deposit it in a closed container which is sent to the laundry daily. Patience, acceptance and encouragement are essential. However, not every adult can cope with this problem. A worker who feels he has reached a limit to his capacity to deal with it should discuss the matter with his supervisor to determine whether anything else could be done to make living more tolerable for himself and the children in the group. In some cases, it may be necessary to transfer the child to another group where there is greater tolerance and ability to deal with this symptom. This should not be considered a serious failing by the worker. The inability to continue to care for a child with serious encopresis must be accepted as an understandable human limitation.

Lying

Lying is prevalent among children in residential treatment. It is a persistent irritant to child care workers because it interferes with orderly group living, contributing to confusion and dissension. As a falsification or denial of truth, lying takes on different forms. Anna Freud (1965, pp. 116-117) classifies lying into three categories:

1. *Innocent lying*: This is exemplified by the very young child who may deny or ignore painful impressions, thus protecting himself from anxiety. Since the anxiety-provoking situation or frustration does not exist in consciousness, it cannot hurt him.

2. *Fantasy lying*: When an older child or adult faces excessive frustration he may cope with the realities which they represent by denial, avoidance or distortion of the truth. This is a regressive form of behavior to avoid intolerable anxiety.

3. *Delinquent lying*: This is resorted to as a defense against a fear of punishment or to gain advantages which a person feels he cannot otherwise achieve. It may also represent an attempt to impress others with a sense of importance which has no basis in reality.

A child may resort to all of these forms at one time or another. However, a psychotic or borderline psychotic child may act as if he is lying when actually he is responding on the basis of his misperception or misconception of reality. He is not consciously falsifying the truth. His "lying," as well as that of children who indulge in "innocent" or "phantasy" lying, should not be dealt with punitively. They are not motivated by a desire to delude, manipulate or exploit others. Emphasis on what is real, to correct misperception, and reassurance, to allay anxiety, are called for.

The basis for delinquent lying may be manifold. Some children simply perpetuate a pattern which they have learned in their own families where not telling the truth was practised as an established mode of interpersonal interaction. Others, especially those who have grown up in disadvantaged neighborhoods, may perpetuate peer patterns which were practiced in order to protect children from adult authority, to avoid punishment for delinquent activities, or to manipulate others for material advantage. Lying may also represent a defense developed in dealing with rigid parental authority; thus a child may lie because he fears severe punishment for the slightest infraction of adult expectations. Lying may also be a manifestation of insecurity in relationships. A child may lie because he believes that he will not be believed when he tells the truth. A feeling of inadequacy may be compensated for by lying or boasting to boost one's sense of adequacy or to impress others and enhance one's status in the peer group. A child may also cheat in competitive situations or games because he feels he cannot achieve on the basis of his own competency.

The child care worker should convey to the children his expectation that they be truthful. They may not be able to comply, but it is a constructive goal to uphold. By his own actions in support of honesty, a child care worker can serve as a model for the children. The destructive consequences of lying should be discussed with the individual child who is involved, or the group as a whole. It is not advisable to use group pressure to expose a child who is lying. It is exploitative of the group as a whole and a manifestation to the children that the child care worker cannot cope with the problem. There should be consequences for delinquent lying and it is advisable to inform the children that if they tell a lie to cover up a transgression they may have additional punishment for lying. Consequences should be enforced to emphasize that the child care worker considers both the offense and the lying about it unacceptable. The child who seems to be a chronic liar should be referred for clinical evaluation and psychotherapeutic treatment intervention.

Stealing

Stealing is destructive to group living and creates serious difficulties for the child care worker. A child who steals poses a threat to the other children who cherish the few possessions they have. The worker is the adult they turn to with complaints about loss, demands for restitution and penalties for the offender. As a guardian of ethical values, the child care worker is concerned about stealing. He may understand the motives of a child's tendency to steal in terms of his personality characteristics and emotional difficulties, but he should not rationalize, excuse, tolerate or disregard theft. The other children view inaction by the child care worker as indirect approval. Understanding why a child steals is important because it helps to formulate intervention techniques to deal with the child as a whole rather than with his symptomatic behavior.

The very young child who does not as yet understand the concept of property will take his playmate's toys openly or will attempt to take an object which attracts him, without inner inhibitions. This cannot be considered stealing. He will gradually learn that this behavior is not acceptable through his parents' instruction. Chronologically, a child in residence might be expected to have learned respect for the possessions of others or at least to be aware of the moral prohibition against theft. This assumption is not always justified. A child who has been reared in a family which either condones or does not disapprove of stealing may continue the family pattern; a child who has been a member of a delinquent peer group may continue the delinquent practices in his cottage; the impulse-ridden child who lacks inner controls will tend to take that which attracts him without inner inhibition; a child driven by compulsive needs to steal (kleptomania) will do so despite the knowledge that it is wrong; the psychotic child may take things that do not belong to him because he cannot differentiate between his or other people's possessions. A socioeconomically deprived child who has grown up in poverty may be tempted to take things from others who are more affluent because he does not want to be different from them nor deprive himself of spending money or money which may be required for outings and trips. The emotionally deprived child's stealing may symptomatically represent his search for substitute satisfaction to fill his loveless void.

The children who consciously steal for personal material gain will require reeducation in values and disciplinary action to discourage stealing. Positive reinforcement in terms of rewards should be offered when they make an effort to control themselves. The impulse-ridden youngster or psychotic child will require patience, as well as growth-inducing nurture, to help him establish inner controls and more adequate judgment of reality. The poverty stricken child should be provided with sufficient material needs so that he does not feel so different from and more deprived than the other children. Finally, the neurotic child will require psychotherapy to resolve the conflicts which express themselves in symptomatic stealing.

The educational component in the treatment effort encompasses the cottage group, the institution as a whole and all the representatives of the disciplines involved in the child's treatment. It is hoped that education in values, as well as psychotherapeutic services, will be available to all the children. Disciplinary action becomes part of the preventive process. When there is a stealing incident and the culprit is identified beyond a reasonable doubt, disciplinary action is necessary. This may include return of the stolen objects or money, restitution through replacement if the object is no longer available, and some degree of deprivation to reinforce the ethical lesson.

A child who steals in neighborhood stores or on shopping trips should be required to return the items to the store, personally, if feasible, and accompanied by a staff member, if possible. A community problem may be created if a youngster steals a car or burglarizes a neighborhood home. He should not be protected from legal action. In these cases, staff, including the child care worker, participate in the legal proceedings in order to interpret his action to the court and, if at all feasible, to request that he be returned for continued treatment.

A child care worker understandably has strong feelings about children in his group who steal. However, theft cannot be considered a personal affront or a failure on his part. Stealing is but one aspect of children's disturbance and must be dealt with therapeutically as any other symptomatic behavior.

Runaways

Institutions have a variety of methods for dealing with runaway children upon their return. These range from welcoming them back with sympathetic understanding that there was good reason for the action, to offering additional attention to demonstrate that they are loved, to warnings of pending punishment for repetition, to severe deprivation in special isolation rooms or "discipline" cottages. The benign approach, often practiced in small residential treatment centers, may be neither acceptable nor applicable in large, heterogeneous institutions or rehabilitation centers for adolescent delinquents where there is administrative concern that to treat a runaway "lightly" may make other children feel that running away "pays off." Large institutions with low staff ratios may also institute harsh deterrents out of concern for the children's safety.

Deprivation of privileges, such as home visits and recreational activities, or additional work assignments are prevalent methods of dealing with returned runaway children. When they

are automatically imposed by edict the results are not necessarily effective. Such consequences may deter some children
but not all. In one institution with a high ratio of runaways,
the usual methods were ineffective until another approach was
instituted to parallel it. A "Runaway Board of Review" consisting of the top administrative personnel from child care, school
and clinic was instituted. It met with each child following his
return. The child had an opportunity to present his reasons
for running away and to hear staff reaction. The seriousness
of his act was emphasized but disciplinary action was left to
the unit administrator. A dramatic reduction in the number
of runaways resulted, principally because the children viewed
this conference as an expression of concern on the part of the
staff. Isolation, excessive or frequently meaningless work activity, extensive deprivation of home visits and leisure time activities seem to be undesirable. These punishments tend to focus
the child's attention on what he considers the unfair consequences imposed upon him, rather than his own actions which
caused it. Feelings of hostility are projected on staff and feelings of rejection are enhanced.

Emphasis should be on prevention. Running away may be
caused by homesickness, disturbing news or a lack of news
from home, a frustrating home visit or an upsetting parental
visit, conflicts within the child and within the group living
situation. It may also be influenced by peer pressures. Child
care workers are well situated to perceive behavior which is
the precursor of running away. A child may seem restless,
show anxiety following receipt of mail from his family or a
friend, or be upset following a parental visit. When anxiety
is evident, the child care worker might comment on the child's
worried appearance and suggest talking about the cause or
arranging for the child to see his caseworker. Where the pre-
cipitating factor in running away is a severe frustrating experience, such as rejection by peers or adults, failure in sport

or school activities, abuse by peers or staff, guilt or fear following the commission of a delinquent act, discussion would have to be supplemented by examination of the situation which caused the action, and determination of appropriate interventions. Running away caused by inducements from another child or a peer group to join them has to be treated differently from running away caused by unsettled conditions in cottage or the institution. Discussion with the children involved may be suitable in the first case; staff evaluation of conditions in the cottage or irritants in the overall program may be essential in the latter case.

Running away is not a constructive way for a child to cope with frustrating situations. The rationale that occasional running away might be good for an inhibited child because it demonstrates assertiveness is faulty. There are more therapeutic and safer ways to help a child handle his conflicts. When a child absconds he exposes himself to damage. He may have an accident, or he may engage in behavior which is delinquent and harmful to himself and to others, or he may be exploited by adults. Girls have frequently been "picked up" by men who exploited them sexually. Time away from the residence also interrupts continuity of treatment.

Although the child care worker may have to administer the imposed punishment, his attitude toward the child must be one of continued acceptance and not of anger for the inconvenience caused or a desire for retribution. Understanding of the runaway should be conveyed, but the act cannot be approved or condoned.

Group discussion can be fruitful in revealing children's thinking and feeling about running away, and can serve to educate them to its hazards. The following is an excerpt from a group meeting following a multiple runaway. It was conducted by a child care supervisor (the author) and a therapist in an older boys' cottage.

Several of the boys began the meeting by telling us how pleased they are about their new cottage parents. They enumerated some of the good qualities which were just the opposite of the negative qualities they had listed when they criticized their former cottage parents.

We saw here an opportunity to introduce the question of running away and to raise the question that if the cottage parents were so good, how could they explain that several of the boys had run away the previous week? There was almost immediate response that it had nothing to do with the cottage parents. Those who had run were "jerks" and they just didn't want to have anything to do with them. We remarked that it might be good to discuss why children ran away. Jim opened the discussion by saying that tensions very often build up and one had to run away from them. Phil immediately counteracted by saying that this was "a lot of baloney." He had never run. Anyway it's only running away from one's self. Jim explained that he never really had a good reason to run away but simply had to do it and then find a rationale for it. Donny seemed quite uncomfortable and wanted to stop the discussion. He said running away is a personal problem and therefore there was no point discussing it in a group. Earlier in his stay, he had run away and got into severe difficulty during the escapades. Fred felt that when there were ambivalent feelings about one's family, and resentment about placement, one was compelled to get away—simply to walk around the streets feeling a little "free" and have time to think. However, at the same time he added that it wasn't very comfortable being a runaway because one was quite insecure about being called "fugitive." Steve agreed, John said that he had run away twice but every time this has set him back in treatment. In fact when one runs away there is a danger one might get hurt. The consensus seemed to be that running away was not advisable but was often necessary. Dave said that sometimes boys run impulsively or because others had run before and it was sort of catching.

When Mr. B., the co-leader, asked the group what they thought our objections were, the boys gave no clear answer and asked us to tell them. We did, reiterating that it interfered with treatment and was risky because many of the boys had poor impulse control. When they ran away they could do things which might hurt themselves and others. The boys agreed. When we mentioned that running away may also be a manifestation of immaturity and incapacity to face one's problems, Burt went over to the window and turned his back to us, Fred took out his lighter and lit pieces of paper in the ash tray and Larry asked to be excused because he wanted to go to the bathroom. When we said that there was nothing to be ashamed of for not having as yet reached maturity, Burt returned to his seat, Fred put out the fire, and Larry relaxed.

CONFIDENTIALITY

There are two aspects of confidentiality. The first has to do with information identifying children. This information should not be divulged to others in conversation, table talk or gossip because it violates a fundamental right of every child to be protected from the dissemination of personal information about him. Neither should staff discuss children in their presence unless they are included as participants in the conversation.

The second aspect relates to confidences conveyed by children. This, too, should be respected unless they involve risks to life and safety or destruction of property. If a child informs a worker that he has something to tell him, but will not do so unless it is kept confidential, then the latter must explain that he cannot keep certain things confidential. He can assure the child that he will help him think it through and also help him decide whether to convey it personally to his caseworker or to administrative persons who must be informed about it. He may offer to do so himself, in the child's presence or without him. To do otherwise and keep the "secret" may represent to the child approval of destructive behavior. For example:

> During his Monday morning therapy session Ben was restless and unusually anxious. He said that he had to tell Mr. S. something very important but could not do so unless he was assured it would be kept confidential. Mr. S. promised and Ben revealed that the previous day he had broken into the school canteen and stolen a large sum of money. The discussion then focused on an examination of the dynamics of the act and what motivated Ben to steal and did not deal with realistic issues such as return of the money and the unreality of keeping this act a "secret." When the theft was discovered during the afternoon, the whole institution was shocked because of the nature of the offense and the scope of the loss. Ben's therapist had kept his promise not to divulge the secret, but Ben subsequently told several of the boys in his cottage. This led to his exposure.

The fact that a child has a need to confide a planned or actual wrongdoing not only indicates that he may want to share it with someone because it troubles him, but also implies that he wants to be prevented from doing something he knows is harmful. This might include running away, suicidal attempts, assaultive acts, setting fires, stealing or destroying property. It is logical to assume that a child would not reveal a "secret" for which he may be punished unless he is masochistically inclined. Revealing it even with the proviso that it be kept confidential implies that the hidden motive is not to conceal the act but to seek intervention.

SEXUAL BEHAVIOR

Sexual behavior includes a broad range of behavior, such as language, gestures, exhibitionism, perversion, individual and group masturbation, homosexuality, and heterosexuality. Viewed from a developmental point of view, it encompasses the life span of an individual. In comparison with other types of behavior, including aggression, sexual behavior in children seems to evoke a great deal of adult anxiety and concern.

Pleasure and curiosity seem to be the motivating forces in children's behavior which is considered sexual. So-called "sexual" behavior is expressed in earliest childhood. Because myelinization of the nervous system (protective sheathing of the nerve fibers) is not complete during the early months of infancy, body areas rich in nerve endings, like the mouth and genitals, are highly sensitive to touch. When the infant discovers that contact with these areas is pleasurable, he tends to perpetuate it. Thus, thumb sucking, and, later on, genital manipulation become sources of pleasure. Our culture accepts thumb sucking as normal in infancy. Genital manipulation is discouraged.

When thumb sucking persists into the second year or beyond, it evokes concern, verbal disapproval, shaming and, not infrequently, physical intervention such as coating the thumb with a bitter solution to discourage the child from this activity. Genital manipulation, now given the status of "masturbation," is reacted to with even greater concern and often with destructive and punitive behaviors by parents. These may range from threats of dire consequences such as illness or body weakness, to physical punishment, evocation of burning in the fires of hell in afterlife, and even castration threats. Parental reactions to such sexual behavior have important emotional consequences and contribute to the determination of the child's attitude regarding sexuality.

The child care worker is frequently faced with children's sexual behavior which, among emotionally disturbed children, is generally exaggerated in form. It may include verbal, homoerotic, homosexual or heterosexual behavior. It may be persistent, aggressive or provocative in expression depending on the nature and degree of the child's disturbance. The worker's therapeutic effectiveness in handling this behavior depends on how he feels about it, which in turn depends on his attitudes regarding sexuality and the extent of knowledge he has about the subject. The manner of handling such behavior should also be adjusted to the type of child who expresses it. Thus, the psychotic child who has poor judgment of reality and little impulse control is less likely to be responsive to "intellectual" discussion regarding his behavior than the child who is fully aware of reality and has sufficient inner controls to modify his behavior following a talk with his child care or social worker.

Thumb Sucking

There is no research evidence that confirms that thumb sucking or masturbation is physically harmful. However, if such behavior persists and is pervasive, it justifies concern because it is symptomatic of difficulties. It may be indicative of conflict regarding sexuality and/or social relationships. The child who persists in sucking his thumb is generally an insecure, emotionally deprived child. When he finds greater security in relationship with others and in activities, whether creative or in sports, it is most likely that thumb sucking will cease because it will no longer be his major source of comfort and pleasure. This will take time, adult patience and support. He will also need protection from ridicule from his own peers as a consequence of this immature behavior.

Masturbation

Unlike thumb sucking, which is generally associated with immaturity rather than sexuality, and which is generally rare beyond early childhood years, masturbation is definitely associated with sexuality and, consequently, evokes a great deal of adult concern.

Most, if not all, children masturbate occasionally. This does not seem problematic to most workers and they tend to ignore it. However, if they find that a child is masturbating excessively or in public areas, in the living room while watching television, or during mealtimes, or if there are reports that he does it in the classroom, it requires attention either through direct intervention or by involving clinical personnel, or both. The worker can deal with this constructively by calling the behavior to the child's attention and explaining to him that it is inappropriate in public. The child's therapist can explore further the meaning of this persistent behavior and the sources which motivate it. Knowledge of the fantasies accompanying masturbation can be helpful for therapeutic planning and intervention.

Mutual masturbation or group masturbation is not infrequent among older children and adolescents. It evokes concern because it may be associated with a belief that, if continued, it may develop into homosexuality. For the most part, this type of behavior is transitory or experimental among preadolescents and adolescents. When witnessed, it should be discouraged by the adult through verbal disapproval or separation of the individuals involved.

Aggression and Sexuality

There is no question about immediate and firm intervention in cases of sexual exploitation of one child by another. If one child is forced by another into masturbation, fellatio, or any other form of sexuality, intervention must be swift and decisive. These are physical and forced assaults from which a child must be protected. Disciplinary action, as well as psychotherapeutic intervention, should follow.

Sexual exploitation is an extreme expression of children's association of sex with aggression. Among disturbed children this fusion results in exaggerated expressive behavior. For example, lewd language and physical gestures may be used to offend peers as well as staff. Outbursts of anger may be accompanied by profanity or sexual references. Sexual gestures or verbal sexual insults may also be utilized to attract attention and provoke shock. In addition, exhibitionism or sexual teasing may be used by either boys or girls as seductive maneuvers toward child care workers or other adults of the opposite sex. Exhibitionism should be handled expeditiously, conveying to the child or children that it is socially unacceptable, that it infringes on the rights of other people and can be upsetting to peers as well as adults. The worker has the opportunity to educate children in social propriety by conveying that sexual expression is a private affair and should not be exhibited in public. He should encourage the child to discuss it with his social worker or therapist so that he can understand the underlying motivation. This may serve to help the child disentangle his distortions of sexual expression as an aspect of aggression.

A child whose life experience has resulted in misconceiving sexuality as aggression may reenact it in play or interpersonal relationships. In play therapy children frequently express their perception of parental sexual activity in terms of aggressive or even assaultive acts by the father on the mother. Others reenact in interpersonally. For example, one day a child care worker had to intervene in a fight between Virginia, a ten-year-old, and her roommate. It was serious, with screaming, hitting, and hair pulling. After the children were separated, Virginia was scolded because she was generally the initiator of fights. When asked why she was fighting this time, she insisted, "We're not fighting. We were practicing for marriage!" The worker was shocked and saddened by such a distorted view of marriage. Apparently Virginia had not witnessed expressions of tenderness between her parents. In families where physical violence is a prevalent mode of expressing anger or hostility or resolving arguments, a child grows up with the notion that this is the way people act (Gardner, 1973, p. 141). Virginia's view of marriage as violent interaction motivated her to prepare for it by fighting with others.

The children may also exhibit their curiosity or conflict about sex by an interest in pornographic literature and pictures. This may be of concern to the worker because of its possible impact on the other children, and should be handled in the same way as situations involving exhibitionism.

Profane Language

Use of profane language is a common occurrence. Most children and adults have at one time or another used swear words or sexually tinged expressions impulsively or as a reaction to a frustrating situation. Since disturbed children have a lower frustration tolerance and greater impulsivity, it is not surprising that they may resort to such expression more frequently. A child who persists in doing so should be told that it is annoying, disrespectful to oneself and others, and unacceptable as a mode of expression.

Children who have grown up in families or neighborhoods where profanity is widely used tend to perpetuate such communication patterns. They will require help through reeducation and identification with other people who use more socially acceptable means of expression. Some younger children who use sexualized phrases may not be aware of their meaning or inappropriateness. For example, Vivian, aged nine, used the phrase "fuck you" persistently. It distressed her child care workers when she responded with this phrase to their "Hello," "Goodnight," or a request to do something. One young worker was particularly infuriated because she perceived it as a hostile, provocative challenge. When it was suggested that this might not be the case, she reacted more calmly to Vivian, talked with her about it, explaining that it was not an appropriate response to a greeting or request, and that its usage was to her disadvantage because it annoyed others. Vivian responded favorably and the phrase gradually faded from her communication.

Excessive use of such sexualized phrases by older boys and girls may represent their immature way of dealing with disturbing situations and interpersonal conflicts. This explanation might be suggested to them along with some appropriate ways of dealing verbally with others. If it persists, they should be dealt with firmly, preferably in calm tones to minimize the secondary satisfaction they may derive from getting their worker upset or making him "lose his cool." It should be made clear that such language will not be tolerated and, if it persists, disciplinary action would be taken.

Teenage language styles change frequently. It may be helpful for child care workers to be familiar with current usage of profane phraseology. For example, Comer and Poussaint (1975, p. 308) point out that the term "motherfucker," which only a few years ago was considered among black youths as an extremely insulting provocation which triggered serious fights, has undergone a transformation in meaning. It is now used by many as a "term of endearment and respect." If a child care worker finds it offensive he should say so and suggest more socially appropriate alternatives. There are also word games which may get out of hand. For example, the "dozens" is a teasing game in which a group of youths provoke each other by inventing sexualized jingles, frequently involving each other's mothers or sisters as the sexual objects. It is a method of discharging tension, a status-seeking banter, and a way of testing one's "toughness." It has resulted in serious fights when the invectives hurled at each other have gone beyond the tolerance of one of the participants. Child care workers should discourage such games in their groups.

Homosexual Behavior

In residential living, overt homosexual behavior can become an unsettling and distressing problem. Even homosexual stimulation evoked by the presence of an effeminate looking boy in an adolescent boys' cottage can cause anxiety, hostility and attacks upon the individual who prompts it. This is exemplified in notes from a group meeting recorded by the author.

Howard, a fragile, effeminate looking intellectual youngster, was admitted on an emergency basis and placed in a cottage with a predominantly aggressive, delinquent oriented group. It was not the most appropriate choice but the only one where a bed was available. Within a few days there were complaints—from Howard that he was being abused and from the other boys that he did not belong in their group. The issue came up when several of the boys began to complain about Howard. He in turn accused some of them of attempting to molest him sexually. Donny said that when he first came to the cottage he was also approached sexually. He had a very hard time but he took it. Izzy added that during the first night after his arrival, some boys came over and asked him to blow them. He told them to "fuck themselves and leave him alone." They did. But Howard doesn't seem to know how to defend himself. He fights with words. Barry said to Izzy, "What do you want from him? It's the only way he knows how to react. He doesn't even know how to fight." I (the group leader) commented that might be true but I was sure if anyone approached Bill with sexual advances he would knock him down or black his eye. Billy nodded in agreement. Someone said, "But Howard doesn't fight back." I said that it seems that he fights back in a way that seems to hurt some boys more than black eyes—with "big words." Some responded, "That's right and we don't like it." Howard waved his hands in excitement, insisting that he wasn't going to take any of this stuff. He was not going to be called a "fag."

Izzy turned to me and said that I had once commented that he seemed to enjoy taunting Howard. He said maybe he does, but actually he's had a tough time too. He isn't so sociable, but he tries to live with others. Howard doesn't know how, and doesn't want to. He just cannot get along with him. There is something about Howard that makes him get angry and he wants to hit him. It had become evident to Mr. B'. the co-leader, and myself that Howard's effeminate innate mannerisms were stimulating the strong homosexual tendencies in many of the boys and they were becoming panicky about their impulses. We looked at each other and felt that we should face the boys with this. Otherwise, there would be serious difficulties afterwards. This seemed the opportune time. Mr. B. remarked that teenage boys have sexual concerns and it was not unusual to have homosexual thoughts and even desires. Perhaps Howard's presence was stimulating such latent feelings and to protect themselves they wanted him out of their sight. Others might be so angry that they want to hurt him, and a few actually did.

This seemed to make a deep impression. The boys looked at each other. Billy laughed, saying, "Remember when I talked about the pool table and shooting out! The

guys started to think immediately in homosexual terms."
(Billy somehow had the knack of hitting the root of many
of the problems that the youngsters were struggling with.)
This evoked laughter among the group. Donny said that
most of them had been faced with something like Howard
faced on admission to the cottage, most of it from boys
who were kidding about homosexual advances. Howard
could not see it as a joke because he takes everything so
seriously. Howard screamed back that he wasn't going to
take it even if it was kidding. I then turned to Howard
and asked him whether there was a possibility that maybe
some of the boys didn't mean what they said and that
they really were kidding him along. He looked a little
puzzled and said, "Maybe."

I then remarked that perhaps Howard had no previous
experience in living with other boys, and maybe it was
hard for him now. Perhaps he could try. Howard sat
down, saying he would give this some thought. But when
Jim said that Howard aggravates them because of his
mannerisms, Howard said with strong emotion: "The
boys accuse me of having a funny grin on my face. Can
I help it if I look this way? I seem to smile but I never
learned to cry, not even when it hurts most." There was
a sudden stillness among the group and then Billy jumped
up and, pointing to Eddie, said that he is the kind of guy
who stands by and lets kids get hurt and doesn't lift a
finger to stop others from doing it. He enjoys torment-
ing Howard and that's why he dislikes him. Eddie
cringed.

Donny got up and said that he is only going to speak
for himself. From now on he is going to leave Howard
alone. He will try to talk to him on his level but if Howard
doesn't respond he's just going to freeze him out and not
talk to him. Phil said, "I'm going to try to give this guy

a break." Several of the other boys said they would do the same. Billy concluded, "You'd better."

Homosexuality is a complex phenomenon. There are numerous theories to explain it, including its source in pathological and faulty family identification, hormonal imbalance and arrest in psycho-sexual development. Homosexuality seems widespread, though society's values oppose it and the overall public attitude toward homosexuals is unaccepting and hostile. Changes in attitude have taken place during the past ten years. There is greater understanding, conveyed through the media of communication, of homosexuality. Although homosexuality is still considered a legal offense in most states, the statutes are not generally enforced. Recently the psychiatric profession declassified homosexuality as a category of mental disorders.

One must guard against the hasty labeling of a child as homosexual. A boy who manifests feminine tendencies, a girl who appears "mannish" or acts tomboyish, or a child who shows preference for close association with members of his own sex is not necessarily homosexual. Research has shown that no more than 10-15% of male homosexuals act or appear effeminate. Our society also differentiates between behavior' which is permissible among females and among males. For example, holding hands, physical closeness or even exchanges of kisses is not considered deviant when it occurs among girls and women. But if boys or men are observed in such activity, they will generally be viewed with suspicion and may be labeled homosexual. In residential settings for emotionally disturbed children it is not infrequent that a child may get into bed with another. This should not be immediately interpreted as sexual behavior, especially if it occurs among younger children. Rather it may demonstrate insecurity and a fear of being alone. Two boys associating closely may be doing so because of insecurity with more extensive relationships or a fear of others.

While they may in the future become involved in sexual behavior together, it is safer not to misjudge them as being homosexual.

Homosexuality is a justifiable description if the following conditions are in evidence: The individual feels sexual desires and sexual responsiveness to members of his own sex; he tends to establish emotional and sexual attachments with members of his own sex; and he finds gratification of his sexual needs only with a partner of the same sex.

Adolescent boys and girls may participate at one time or another in experimentation with homosexual behavior but this does not mean that they are, or may become, confirmed homosexuals. It may indicate confusion, as well as a search for sexual identity. In this process they may submit to sexual seduction by a member of the same sex, or involve themselves in limited individual or group experimentation.

In residential living overt homosexual behavior in a cottage group cannot be condoned because of its threat to group stability. If it involves forced seduction, its consequences on the individual child may be traumatic. It may evoke extreme anxiety among children who may be confused about their own sexuality or have latent homosexual tendencies. The child care worker can exercise a degree of control over the overt manifestations of homosexuality. The simplest approach, not necessarily the most effective, is to disapprove of or stop the overt acting out immediately. Incidents should be immediately called to the attention of administrative and clinical personnel for therapeutic planning and intervention.

Heterosexual Behavior

In residential settings that serve both male and female adolescents, heterosexual acting out may become a problem. It is a justified area of concern. Institutions do not function in a vacuum outside of greater society. They reflect societal attitudes towards adolescent sexuality. The community expects conformity to prevailing sexual values of society. Residents, like their peers outside, are subject to the same pressures and contradictions which lead to conflicts, confusion and sexual acting out. Among these are contradictory adult teaching or preaching ranging from rigid prohibition to outright permissiveness, peer pressures and seductions, and stimulation via mass communication media such as television, movies and pornographic literature.

Sexual acting out in the institution may also be an indication of intrapsychic conflicts which are expressed interpersonally in sexual activity. For the most part, young people who require residential treatment have not experienced wholesome family or peer relationships. Consequently, they may have developed distortions, ambivalence, anxiety and conflict about sexuality. Those who have acted out sexually may attempt to perpetuate such behavior by involving other youngsters. This presents serious difficulties in a co-ed institution. Both the perpetrator and the follower may need help in overcoming impulsive or defensive sexual tendencies.

The therapeutic environment, consisting of the structure, which designates rules of conduct, and the staff, representing significant relationships to the young people, should provide guideposts for change toward greater emotional health and maturation. Rules concerning appropriate sexual conduct without support from significant persons who represent and monitor them do not guarantee control of unacceptable behavior, and certainly are not very effective in helping the young people internalize constructive values. Rules and guidelines clearly communicated do provide a protection for those who are unable to resolve internal conflicts about sex. They provide a shelter from anxiety for those who are not yet ready to assume responsibility for determining their own standards of sexual behavior. The staff's sensitivity and skill in dealing with the sexual conflicts of youth are of importance. The degree of their conviction about established regulations concerning sexual behavior does not escape the residents. The genuineness of their own value system concerning sexuality is readily perceived by the children. Staff is judged by their actual rather than their professed values and behavior. The youngsters will more readily be influenced by the "real" rather than the professed values. If they discover that an adult does not practice what he preaches, they consider him hypocritical, justifying their alienation from adult values.

Co-ed activities require adult supervision because many of the boys and girls are easily stimulated to act out sexually. Creativity and ingenuity are required in planning dances, outings and parties. Inconspicuous but alert adult presence is essential to assure that these activities remain pleasant socializing experiences for all children rather than arenas for sexual stimulation and impulsive acting out.

The latter circumstances is illustrated by the following:

> During a co-ed party hosted by a girls' cottage, some of the children requested permission to watch a television program. One of the girls, Joan, insisted that all lights be out. Despite some misgivings, staff acceded. During the program, a number of the girls seemed restless and upset. After the party was over, the girls accused Joan of manipulating staff and her peers to agree to darkness so she could pet with her boyfriend. They felt exploited and accused her of "spoiling" what could have been a very nice party. The recriminations, denials, tears and shouting resulted in a highly upset group of girls and a distressed staff. It seemed that staff indecisiveness and ambivalence about implementing a supervisory function had turned a pleasant co-ed party into an unpleasant experience for

children and staff. Joan's sexual activity had evoked anxiety from the other girls. All of this could have been avoided if staff had refused Joan's request. It was logical to do so because there was a rule about keeping a TV light on during television viewing. A child care worker could have said, "Sorry, Joan, you know the rules. It is not good to watch television in darkness because it is damaging to the eyes." The girls, including Joan, would have had to accept this because they were aware of the established practice, and thus Joan's manipulation and her acting out, as well as the impact on the group, could have been avoided.

Sex Education Program

Child care workers should be well informed and secure about their own attitudes regarding sexuality in order to help the children in this area. They should be an integral part of a comprehensive sex education program involving children as well as staff. One such program in a foster care agency addressed itself first to staff in order to develop their competency in conveying sex information to the children and to enable them to deal more constructively with children's sexual behavior. The first phase of the program consisted of sessions led by medical personnel which presented to staff factual information. This included anatomy, pubescent development in boys and girls, menstruation, pregnancy, abortion and venereal diseases. A psychiatrist talked with the group about sexual deviation, including excessive masturbation, homosexuality, and promiscuity. The second phase focused on staff attitudes and values. These were discussed in small groups, including social workers and child care workers. Examples from daily child care practice were the basis for discussion. Values and personal attitudes were discussed, reaction to children's sexual behavior was examined, and methods of dealing with it worked out. This prepared the staff for the most important phase of the sex education program—conveying sex education to children and dealing with their sexual behavior. Group meetings were held and, at children's requests, medical personnel joined sessions to present sex information and to answer children's questions. Subsequently, more of the children were able to bring their questions and concerns to staff, especially to child care workers. The atmosphere of receptivity came across to the children and they felt more comfortable in talking about these matters with staff.

Child care workers emphasized that the group discussion had made them more aware of their own attitudes regarding sexuality. This was helpful in guiding children toward more constructive values. However, the road to self-awareness was not always an easy one, as exemplified by the following:

> During a staff discussion about masturbation, Bill, a young child care worker, expressed a very liberal attitude. He felt that children who masturbated excessively were troubled. When they did so in public they should not be reprimanded as "bad" or punished. It was best to tell them that their behavior was inappropriate in the presence of others.
>
> When Bill came to the next group discussion, he seemed distressed and asked to speak first. He said that something happened the night before which made him feel ashamed because he had mishandled a child. He had walked into the living room where the children were watching television, and noted that Jimmy was masturbating. His immediate response was to shout at the child "What the hell do you think you are doing?" Jimmy had cringed at the onslaught. Bill immediately realized that he had acted impulsively and unfairly. He questioned

why he had reacted in this manner when the week before
he had discussed such a situation entirely from a different
point of view. He realized there was still a gap between
his intellectual understanding and his deeply ingrained
feelings and attitudes. There were still vestiges of his
childhood upbringing in a Fundamentalist Protestant
family where he and his siblings were indoctrinated about
sins related to sex. Masturbation was considered a serious
transgression which would be severely punished here and
in the hereafter. Now that he is conscious of the connection between his impulsive reaction to Jimmy and his
early indoctrination, he feels that he can handle himself
differently in the future.

HEALTH CARE

The child care worker plays an important role in protecting
children's physical well-being. He supervises and guides them
in maintaining standards of personal cleanliness and grooming,
eating well balanced meals to assure adequate nutritional
needs, physically exercising through recreational activities, and
wearing clothing appropriate to weather conditions. He has to
be alert to signs of illness or side effects of medication, sensitive to children's physical complaints, and ready to act quickly
when a child becomes ill suddenly or sustains an injury. The
child care worker's contact with agency medical staff is generally limited to the nurse(s), but in the nurse's absence he
may have to contact a doctor or take a child to a hospital
emergency room. He is also expected to be familiar with established medical procedure, which he is expected to follow
as needed. The following abstract from the medical procedures
of a residential treatment center (Childville, 1976) exemplifies
such directives:

Children should be observed for any unusual signs of illness, i.e., colds, cuts, bruises, nosebleeds, swellings, rashes, etc., and brought to the attention of the nurse. Any abnormality is to be referred to the nurse immediately.

Children should be ready for clinics on time and should be appropriately dressed.

All illness or emergencies should be called to the nurse's attention when she is on duty.

In the absence of the nurse or nurse's assistant, Dr. D............, telephone no. ...., is to be called in all cases of illness. This means if a child has an elevated temperature; if he complains of any aches or pains; if he vomits more than once, has a cough, etc.

If a child sustains injury of any kind, falls, or has pains that might indicate internal injury, has sprain or fracture, contact nurse or doctor. In their absence, take child to .... Hospital Emergency Clinic.

STANDING ORDERS

1. *For minor cuts or scrapes,* wash with soap and water, apply a small amount of bacitracin ointment and a bandaid.
2. *For major cuts or lacerations,* cover with sterile gauze and take child to hospital emergency room.
3. *For a cold,* child should be kept indoors, at rest, and encouraged to drink fluids. Temperature should be checked morning and later afternoon. If cold symptoms are very discomforting, a teaspoon of Dimetapp Elixir may be given three times a day. Should a child's sleep be interrupted by coughing, a teaspoon of Cheracol D-M may be given. This may be repeated only once during the night.
4. *For fever* (rectal temperatures above 101°), call the answering service to report to the doctor. Should the temperature rise rapidly and cause discomfort, while awaiting the doctor's instructions, give one tablet Tylenol every four hours as needed. For rectal temperatures between 100° and 101° the child should be observed unless there is

abdominal pain or severe headache, in which case doctor should be called.

5. *For headache,* put child to rest in bed and check temperature. If there is fever, follow directions as in item 4 above.

6. *For sore throat,* check temperature. Without fever, if associated with cold symptoms, follow procedure as in item 3 above.

7. *For abdominal pain* that persists, note other symptoms such as vomiting or diarrhea, temperature, and report to doctor.

8. *For nausea or vomiting* without abdominal pain, give nothing by mouth for three or four hours. Child may be allowed to suck on ice or hard candy. When nausea and vomiting stop, give teaspoonful of any of the following clear liquids every 20 minutes: coca cola, ginger ale, fruit juice. As child improves, these fluids may be increased in amount slowly. If nausea and vomiting recur, stop all fluids and repeat as above. If vomiting continues, notify doctor.

9. *For diarrhea,* stop all food except the following: rice, skim milk, banana, pot cheese, farmer cheese, skim milk cottage cheese, dry toast, saltine crackers, clear broth, orange juice, Dezerta gelatin. Give two teaspoons of Kaopectate following each loose bowel movement.

10. *For nose bleed,* keep child in sitting position with head tilted forward over a sink or basin. Pinch nose on the affected side or sides very firmly and continuously for five minutes. During this time, child will be breathing through his mouth. Should nose bleed continue or recur, repeat this process. Do not pack nose, do not apply cold compresses.

11. *For burns,* immerse part in cold water or apply cold wet compresses. Dry gently and apply Bacitracin ointment and cover with sterile gauze dressing and bandage roll. Tape may be applied on outside of bandage roll. If there is

blistering or raw areas of skin, follow same procedure and report to doctor.

12. *For head injuries* associated with loss of consciousness of repeated vomiting, take child to emergency room of ....Hospital.

13. *For injuries to extremities* where normal motion is limited or normal weight bearing is not possible, take child to emergency room of........................Hospital.

14. *For toothache,* give Tylenol, apply cold compress externally, and rinse mouth with lukewarm water every half-hour. Check temperature, and if elevated, call doctor.

15. *For rashes associated with severe itching,* give Benadryl Elixir, 1 teaspoon 4 times daily.

16. *For eye problems:*
    a) All cases of eye injury with pain should be taken to emergency room of........................Hospital.
    b) For foreign body in eye, take child to emergency room of........................Hospital.
    c) For eye discharge, compress eye with warm water (use cotton balls).

17. *For earache,* check temperature, give Tylenol and call answering service of doctor.

All temperatures should be taken rectally.
If any of the above occur, please indicate this in the log book.

MEDICATION

Medication is prescribed for the relief of excessive anxiety and control of impulsive behavior. The over-anxious child is unable to cope with the requirements of daily living; the impulsive child is constantly in difficulty because, lacking sufficient inner controls, he cannot adapt to the requirements of social living. Both experience inner turmoil and outer frustration because they cannot concentrate on work or learning and their behavior often results in social rejection.

Prescription of medication is a psychiatric responsibility. The five major categories of medication for children (Nichtern, 1973, pp. 43-59) include the following:

1. *Tranquillizers* such as *Thorazine, Mellaril* and *Stelazine* are *phenothiazines.* They are sedating, relieve anxiety and decrease impulsivity. Thorazine and Mellaril are generally prescribed for the agitated child; Stelazine seems more effective with the depressed and withdrawn child. These phenothiazines have been found to be most effective in treating disturbances of childhood and adolescence associated with the schizophrenias. *Librium* and *Valium* are considered milder forms of tranquillizers than the phenothiazines. They are useful in reducing tension and anxiety evoked by distressful situations. *Benadryl* seems effective for the young hyperactive and impulsive child.

2. *Stimulants,* including *amphetamines* such as *Benzedrine, Dexedrene* and *Ritalin,* given in proper doses, have a calming effect on children, whereas they produce stimulating "highs" in adults. The amphetamines make the hyperactive child quieter and more relaxed, decrease mood swings, improve attention span and relieve tension. They seem most effective with children who have neurotic problems which are expressed in hyperactive behavior. Ritalin is effective in children diagnosed as having minimal brain dysfunction or whose behavior is characterized by distractibility, impulsivity, hyperactivity, specific learning disabilities and perceptual impairment.

3. *Antidepressants* such as *Elavil* and *Tofranil* are used for relief of symptoms of depression, and depression accompanied by anxiety. This includes restlessness,

sleep disturbance, phobias. Tofranil has also proven to be effective in controlling enuresis in children.

4. *Sedatives: Barbiturates* are not generally prescribed for children because they tend to decrease alertness and loosen controls. However, they are used as behavior modifying agents for brain-damaged children.

5. *Anti-convulsants* such as *Dilantin* help control seizure reactions.

There may be adverse side effects depending on the type of drug used. Children seem to be less affected than adults. When side effects occur, they can be modified quickly by changing dosage. The child care worker should be aware of these physical manifestations, and when observed they should be quickly reported to the child's caseworker or the psychiatrist who prescribed the medication.

Some of the major *side effects* are:

1. *Thorazine:* Drowsiness, usually mild to moderate, may occur, particularly the first or second week, after which it generally disappears. Jaundice may appear between the second and fourth week of therapy. It is usually reversible on withdrawal of medication. There may be allergic reactions, especially to sunlight, occasional dry mouth, nasal congestion, constipation and sore throat.

2. *Mellaril:* Drowsiness tends to subside with continued medication or a reduction in dosage. There may be dryness of mouth, blurred vision, nausea, jaundice and occasional tremors of limbs.

3. *Tofranil:* Hypertension, tingling of extremities, dry mouth, blurred vision, urinary retention, rash and nausea may occur.

4. *Stelazine:* Drowsiness, dizziness, skin reaction, rash, dry mouth, insomnia, fatigue may occur.
5. *Ritalin:* Restlessness and insomnia are the most common adverse reactions initially, but are usually controlled by reducing dosage and omitting the drug in the afternoon or evening.
6. *Valium:* Side effects most commonly reported are drowsiness, fatigue and sleep disturbance.
7. *Elavil:* Disturbed concentration, hypertension, dry mouth, blurred vision, skin rash may occur.

DRUG ABUSE

Many children in residence have been affected by abuse of drugs, including alcohol, either by exposure in their families or neighborhoods, by actual experimentation or by extensive usage. Involvement with drugs results from a diversity of influences and motivations—curiosity, a desire to be accepted by peers, defiance or rebelliousness against adult values, a manifestation of inner conflicts or more serious disturbance.

The extensive use of drugs has deleterious effects upon the physical and/or psychological well-being of the user. Certain drugs create an actual physical dependence (addiction) and painful withdrawal symptoms occur upon discontinuance. A broad range of psychological effects, varying from mildly to euphorically pleasant sensations and experiences to disruptive, extremely anxiety-arousing reactions, are possible. Acute panic and profound anxiety leading to psychotic episodes necessitating hospitalization are not uncommon. Reliance on drugs to enable one to "feel good" is an avoidance of responsibility and of facing reality. It may reflect underlying personality disturbance. Preadolescents and adolescents who become involved in drug use are more vulnerable to the various harmful influences of drugs than adults because of the unusual stresses associated with this tumultuous stage of development.

The child care worker is in a crucial position in drug control and prevention programs in the institution. His close proximity to the children enables him to note behavior which may be related to drug usage. He should be sufficiently knowledgeable to recognize drug symptoms and to convey to children the dangers of drug usage. Following are guidelines for identifying drug usage.

Drug Identification and Consequences of Usage (Taxel, 1970)

1. *Glue sniffing:*

    Physical symptoms include drunken appearance, dreamy or blank expression and violent actions.

    Objects associated with usage are tubes of glue, large paper bags or handkerchiefs.

    If used extensively, there is danger of damage to lung, brain and liver, and of death through suffocation or choking.

2. *Marijuana,* known also as "pot," "grass," "Mary Jane," "hashish," "reefers," "tea":

    Physical symptoms include drowsiness, wandering mind, enlarged pupils, lack of coordination, craving for sweets and increased appetite.

    Objects associated with usage include strong odor of burnt leaves, small seeds in pocket lining, cigarette paper, discolored fingers.

Although varied authorities have indicated that excessive use of marijuana may result in psychological dependence and inducement to use more harmful drugs, lethargy or some physical damage, this is not as yet clearly confirmed by research findings. Results of studies have not been definitive or consistent, and are often contradictory.

3. *Hallucinogens:* L.S.D., also known as "Acid," "Sugar Cubes," "trips," D.M.T. and S.T.P.

Physical symptoms include severe hallucinations, feelings of detachment, incoherent speech, cold hands and feet, vomiting, hysterical laughing and crying.

Objects associated with usage include cube sugar with discoloration in center, strong body odor, small tubes of liquid.

Dangers include suicidal tendencies, unpredictable behavior. Chronic exposure causes brain damage.

4. *Amphetamines,* also known as "Bennies," "Dexies," "Poppers," "Pep Pills," "Lip Poppers," and "Wake-Ups," and *Methamphetamines* ("Speed," "Dyna-mite")

Physical symptoms, include aggressive behavior, giggling, silliness, rapid speech, confused thinking, no appetite, extreme fatigue, dry mouth, shakiness, insomnia.

Objects associated with usage are pills or capsules of varying colors, chain smoking.

Dangers associated with usage include death from overdose, hallucinations, psychotic episodes.

5. *Barbiturates,* also known as "barbs," "blue devils," "yellow jackets," "candy," "phennies," "goof balls," "downs"

Physical symptoms include drowsiness, stupor, dullness, slurred speech, drunken appearance, vomiting.

Objects associated with usage are pills or capsules of varying colors.

Dangers include death or unconsciousness from overdose, addiction, convulsions in withdrawal.

6. *Heroin,* also known as "horse," "scat," "junk," "snow," "stuff," "Harry," "joy powder."

Morphine, "white stuff," "dreamer," "Miss Emma." *Codeine,* "schoolboy."

Physical symptoms include stupor, drowsiness, needle marks on body, watery eyes, loss of appetite, blood stain on shirt sleeve, running nose.

Objects associated with usage include needle or hypodermic syringe, cotton, tourniquet-string, rope, belt, burnt bottle caps or spoons, glassine envelopes.

Dangers include death from overdose, addiction, liver and other infections due to unsterile needles.

7. *Cough Medicine containing Codeine and Opium*

Physical symptoms include drunken appearance, lack of coordination, confusion, excessive itching.

Object associated with usage is an empty bottle of medicine.

There are *dangers if used extensively;* the most serious is addiction.

Counteraction

Upon discovery of any drug usage by an individual child or group of children, or the circulation of drugs in the group, the worker should report it immediately to his supervisor. Drug use may raise the level of anxiety in the group as a whole because children may become aware of its use by one or more peers before staff discovers it. These clues should be followed up. Some children may bring drugs from home visits. The kind of action to be taken regarding an individual child using drugs will be dependent on agency policy. It may range from treatment based on clinical assessment, or disciplinary measures, or both, to temporary transfer to a drug treatment facility, or removal from care.

Child care workers should be involved in drug education programs. When a drug incident occurs, group discussion about it is called for and should be initiated by the workers.

RECORDING OBSERVATIONS

The "case record" generally refers to recording by clinical staff, namely social workers, psychiatrists and psychologists, and rarely contains recorded material by child care workers. When there are references to a child's behavior in his living group, it is generally secondhand reporting recorded by caseworkers.

There is value in child care recording. Its immediate importance is communication of information about an individual child or the group among child care staff who work different shifts. This contributes to greater continuity and consistency in dealing with the children. It is also useful in conveying information to other members of the residential team—caseworkers, psychiatrists and teachers. The form and content of the child care record differ depending on the requirements of the institution, time available and the manpower resources to achieve it. Recording may simply be a daily log with brief entries regarding individual children or group behavior, which may be supplemented by concise or even process recording of crisis situations. The following are examples of log entries:

5/20/75—8:00 P.M. Jimmy was in good shape today. He functioned well in school, got along with all the children and staff.

5/22/75—9:00 A.M. Fay was upset this morning, was irritable with everyone, refused to eat breakfast or do her chores and cried before going to school. Informed caseworker who will see her today.

5/25/75—5:00 P.M. Michael was out of control after return from home visit. He started a fight with David and had to be isolated in his room for an hour until he calmed down. Refused to tell me what troubled him.

The recording of crises is important because it provides ongoing follow-up by other disciplines. The following illustrates the importance of recording a critical incident.

On Sunday evening following return from a Thanksgiving visit with her mother, Melissa was restless, annoyed the other children and was unresponsive to my efforts to control her. When Mrs. M. entered the cottage living room, Melissa assaulted her physically, calling her abusive names. Together, we had to physically restrain her and remove her from the room.

This entry, read by the workers who came on duty the following morning, alerted them to the need to deal with Melissa's disturbance. Promptly conveyed to the child's caseworker, it helped clarify what had occurred to precipitate the outburst. Melissa had had a highly disappointing visit with her mother, who had neglected her in favor of her lover. Apparently Melissa was very angry but could not express it while at home. Subsequently she acted out her frustration, first toward her peers and then in the attack against the child care worker. Her perceptions had become so blurred by the traumatic experiences at home that when Mrs. M. walked into the room, Melissa perceived her to be her mother. The attack was a manifestation by a borderline psychotic child at a time of stress when her perception of reality was blurred. Her anger with her mother was misplaced upon another women whom she knew and liked but who resembled her mother (in color only). The workers had not known the facts of the home visit but had sensed that the violent outburst on Melissa's part was not a personal attack, but an irrational outburst by a very disturbed child.

No matter what the form the recording takes, it should be clear and concise. In selective situations requiring process recording, it is important that recording be done daily and that time be made available.

REFERENCES

ADLER, JACK, "The Child Care Counsellor as 'Target of Transferred Behavior'." *Child Care Quarterly*, July, 1973.

ADLER, JACK, Editor, *Hawthorne Cedar Knolls Schools Clinic Manual.* 1963 (mimeographed).

ADLER, JACK and FINKEL, WILLIAM, "Integrating Remedial Methods into Child Care Practice." *Child Care Quarterly*, Vol. 5. No. 1, 1976.

ADLER, JACK, "Interpersonal Relationships in Residential Treatment Centers for Disturbed Children." *Child Welfare*, Vol. 50, No. 4, 1971, pp. 208-217.

ALTERMAN, JOHN, *Child Care with an Aggressive Child*. Pleasantville Cottage School, N.Y., 1973 (unpublished paper).

American Psychiatric Association, *A Psychiatric Glossary.* Washington, D.C., 1964.

BEKER, JEROME, GITLESON, PAUL M., KAMINSTEIN, PHILIP and ADLER, LOIS FINKEL, *Critical Incidents in Child Care.* New York, Behavioral Publications, 1970.

Childville—*Health Care Policy*, 1976, mimeographed.

COMER, JAMES P. and POUSSAINT, ALVIN F., *Black Child Care.* New York, Simon & Schuster, 1975.

DIAMOND, ANDREW, *Child Care Orientation Manual.* Pleasantville Cottage School, 1973 (unpublished).

Edenwald School *Manual of Policies and Procedures*, 1974, mimeographed.

ENGLISH, SPURGEON O. and PEARSON, GERALD J., *Emotional Problems of Living.* New York, W.W. Norton, 1945.

FOSTER, G. W., VANDERVEN, K. D., KRONER, E. R., CARBONARA, N. T. and COHEN, G. N., *Child Care with Emotionally Disturbed Children.* Pittsburgh, University of Pittsburgh Press, 1972.

FREUD, ANNA, *Normality and Pathology in Childhood.* New York, International Universities Press, 1965.

GARDNER, RICHARD A., *Understanding Children.* New York, Jason Aronson, 1973.

HIRSCHFIELD, ERIC and STARR, JULIA, "The Contribution of the Volunteer to the Program of a Children's Institution." In *Healing Though Living*, Mayer, Morris F. and Blum, Arthur, editors, Springfield, Ill., Charles C Thomas, 1971, pp. 94-108.

KING, CHARLES H., "The Ego and the Integration of Violence in Homicidal Youth." *American Journal of Orthopsychiatry*, 45(1), Jan., 1975, pp. 134-145.

KING, CHARLES H., "Countertransference and Counter-Experience in the Treatment of Violence-Prone Youth." *American Journal of Orthopsychiatry*, 46(1), Jan., 1976, pp. 43-61.

LEMAY, MICHEL, *The Functions of the Specialized "Educateur" for Maladjusted Youth.* English translation by Vivian Jarvis, Green Chimneys School, Brewster, N.Y., November, 1974 (mimeographed.

MENNINGER, KARL, *New York Times*, 10/30/68.

NICHTERN, SOL, "Psychopharmacotherapy for Children." *Pediatric Annals*, Vol. 2, No. 3, 1973, pp. 43-59.

PIERCE, CHESTER M., "Enuresis." In *Comprehensive Textbook of Psychiatry*, Freedman, Alfred M. and Kaplan, Harold L., editors, Baltimore, Williams and Wilkins, 1967, pp. 1380-1383.

REDL, FRITZ *When We Deal with Children.* New York, The Free Press, 1966.

TAXEL, I., *Narcotics Identification Guide.* Woodmere, N.Y., 1970.

TREISCHMAN, ALBERT E., "Understanding the Stages of a Temper Tantrum." In *The Other 23 Hours*, Treischman, Albert E., Whittaker, James K. and Brendtro Larry K., editors, Chicago, Aldine, 1969.

WHITTAKER, JAMES K., "Managing Wake-Up Behavior." In *The Other 23 Hours*, Treischman, Albert E., Whittaker, James K. and Brendtro, Larry K., editors, Chicago, Aldine, 1969.

WOLSTEIN, BENJAMIN, *Transference*. New York, Grune and Stratton, 1954.

4. Relationships

SEPARATION

During the course of a child's growth, separation experiences are inevitable and necessary for maturation and individuation. Although each new step of separate functioning entails anxiety for the very young child, the mother's availability, love and support minimize anxiety and make the process of achieving individuation pleasurable. Under these circumstances, separation experiences are viewed as essential and constructive (Mahler and La Perriere, 1965). Precipitous, long-term or repeated separations have been found to be destructive to children.

The emotional implications of separation permeate placement from its beginning through termination. Separation affects both the child who is placed and his family. Child care workers inevitably become involved with children's and parents' reactions to separation and its manifestations during placement.

Children's Reactions

Children's reactions to separation vary (Littner, 1960). Most children experience a sense of abandonment. They may

147

feel helpless because they have no control over what is happening to them, and "worthless" because of feeling that if they were worthy, their parents would not have placed them. They may blame themselves for offenses which have no basis in reality. They may not only consider themselves "bad," but also view placement as punishment for their behavior. Their feelings of guilt and anger may be repressed, with resulting anxieties and emergence of neurotic symptoms.

The placed child may react with displacement of emotions. He may expect staff attitudes and behavior to be similar to those he experienced in his family, school and neighborhood. He may view staff as the people who will punish him for imagined or actual sins. Expecting punishment, he may protect himself by "attacking" first or by withdrawing into isolation. A child who is masochistically inclined may try to evoke punishment to allay guilt feelings. A child may also hesitate to establish close and significant relationships with adults because of the fear that if he loves them or is loyal to them his own parents will resent it, or because of a feeling that he will again be rejected and subjected to another separation. Similar reactions may be expressed in relation to other children in the group.

The older child in placement, especially the adolescent, faces additional difficulties. The general instabilities which pervade adolescence are aggravated by separation. Intensified feelings of ambivalence toward parents may then be nourished by actual or fantasized feelings of parental rejection. The resolution of the dependence-independence conflict becomes more complex and difficult. Negative feelings are more readily displaced or projected. Child care workers are drawn into the vortex of the emotional turmoil that accompanies the strivings for independence. They may become the object of defiance and rebelliousness, rationalized by such expressions as "You can't tell me what to do. You are not my parents!"

Orienting the Newcomer

The impact of separation on the newly admitted child should not be minimized. The outward lack of concern may simply be a defense to control inner anxiety. Child care workers require preparation for the new arrival. The greater their understanding, the better equipped they will be to cope constructively with the child's feelings about leaving his home, friends and neighborhood. Upon admission, the child finds himself to be a stranger in the group. The other children should have been prepared for his arrival. However, with the best of preparation, it is not certain how they will react to him. Some may view him as an intruding sibling, others may exploit him, some may tolerate him and some may accept him. The child care worker helps him become acquainted with all the children, and specifically with those children who will be ready to befriend him and help him adapt to the climate and to the expectations of the peer group. The worker also orients him to routines, rules and expectations of the center and introduces him to the various programs. The worker's availability should be assured him as needed.

Parental Feelings

Feelings about separation permeate all families and affect all family members (Adler 1970). Fathers and mothers, siblings and relatives, may be shaken by the fragmentation of family cohesiveness as a result of placement of one or more of its children. Feelings of guilt and anger generated by inner conflicts are intensified by outside pressures. Prevalent community attitudes are generally not sympathetic to parents who place their children. They are not considered adequate persons or "good" parents. Consequently, their own guilt feelings and sense of failure as parents become intensified. These may be further reinforced by residential staff who convey to the chil-

dren indirectly, by implication, or directly by word, deed or
derogatory attitudes that they are "rescuing" or "protecting"
them from their "irresponsible" parents (Mandelbaum 1962).
This may evoke counter-hostility on the part of the parents,
who may then react in ways which are destructive to their
children's adjustment.

Observations

Following admission and subsequently as appropriate, the
worker should report his observation of a child's reaction to
separation to his caseworker:

1. Does he seem to be homesick (cries easily when
   family is mentioned, when he receives mail or a telephone call from home)?
2. Does he say he prefers being here to being at home?
3. Does he engage worker in frequent talks about his
   home and family members?
4. Does he seem not to accept placement, refusing to
   cooperate with institutional requirements?
5. Has he made an adjustment to cottage living, his peers
   and workers, but sporadically expresses a desire to be
   at home, indicating ambivalence about placement?

RELATIONSHIPS WITH INDIVIDUAL CHILDREN

From the moment of arrival, a child finds himself in a
planned, controlled environment, a group living situation, with
a broad spectrum of relationships with peers and adults. He is
confronted by unfamiliar interpersonal situations to which he
will have to adapt. The prospect evokes uncertainties and anxieties even among relatively well-adjusted children. It can be
frightening and threatening to the handicapped disturbed child.
In extreme cases, there may be regression to earlier, more im-

mature modes of behavior, with troublesome consequences to residential staff (Adler, 1971).

The new resident cannot readily divest himself of fixed attitudes and anxieties that have guided his interpersonal relationships in the past. Lacking basic trust in himself and in others, he approaches new relationships with reservations and suspicions. Before he will permit himself to trust adults, he may test them to the limits of their patience. All staff is subject to this process but child care workers are particular targets. Since they spend many hours daily with the children, they represent important and meaningful adults. As already indicated they may take on the attributes of parents or other significant persons who may have hurt and disappointed the children. Therefore, they may become objects of a child's projected and displaced distortions and the targets of transferred emotions. The worker must be aware of this in order to avoid destructive counter-reactions which will hinder the establishment of positive relationships between the child and himself. (Projections and displacement are psychic processes, operating unconsciously. In projection, unacceptable feelings are attributed to others. In displacement, emotions are displaced from the original object to a more accepted substitute.)

Communication Problems

Child care workers are faced with difficult communication problems in their working relationships with emotionally disturbed children. The children's verbal statements are not always the complete message. The form, nuances of expression, subtle nonverbal postures and behavior may contain the most significant elements of interpersonal communication. These, more than the words the child uses, reflect his developmental level, family life-style and cultural background. They may also represent transference reactions. Unless the worker is able to decode the totality of a child's communication, the message cannot be fully understood, and the establishment of a positive relationship between child and worker is endangered, since the child does not feel he is understood and the worker's response may be inappropriate and viewed as hostile. Consequently, a capacity to listen, to observe, to understand the child's communication and to convey this to him through specific and appropriate verbal responses is essential. An awareness of his own reactions is also desirable because the child also reacts to the totality of the worker's communication, including nonverbal cues.

Meaning of Relationship

Most children in residential treatment have not developed sufficient ego strengths to enable them to control inner impulse pressures and to tolerate frustration. Like the young child who in the process of socialization learns to postpone impulse gratifications by giving in to his parents' demands in order to gain their approval, the child in residential treatment interacts similarly with significant persons in his daily living. This process will have a chance of success if he is able to establish relationships with adults who represent accepting, caring and firm, benign authority. We find Brendtro's definition of relationship appropriate. He states that establishing a relationship with disturbed or maladjusted children consists of three components: increasing the child's communication with the adult, increasing the child's responsiveness to social reinforcement provided by the adult, and increasing the tendency of the child to model the behavior of adults (Brendtro, 1969, p. 54).

Alice and Danny illustrate the influence of significant relationships upon antisocial youngsters:

> Alice, age 13½, looked and acted like a street urchin. She did not attend school, associated with undesirable companions and was not controllable by her parents.

Upon admission from Family Court she was shabbily dressed in boys dungarees and shirt, was unkempt, ragged and dirty. She came from a severely deprived working-class family and grew up in a home sparsely furnished with broken furniture. She was sulky and unfriendly. Unbeknown even to herself, she was endowed with high intelligence, sensitivity, artistic talent and capacity for relationships. Within a year she became intrigued by her caseworker and an art teacher who expressed a genuine interest in her. She began to paint and displayed a great talent, wrote highly sensitive poetry and became seriously involved in therapy. She modified her asocial attitudes and modeled her behavior on the people who had become significant to her. Her life outlook and self-image changed dramatically by the time she left the institution at the age of 17.

Danny, a child reared in a disorganized, economically impoverished family living in a deteriorated neighborhood, had become delinquent at an early age. He was hostile to authority, uninterested in education and pleasure oriented. He resisted treatment and soon became a domineering leader in the peer culture. His gradual attachment to the school principal, a physically impressive man who took an interest in Danny and could cope with his persistent provocation without becoming hostile, modified his attitude toward adults. He admired the principal and became devoted to him. He seemed to have found an ideal replacement for his irresponsible delinquent father who had deserted the family years before. As a consequence, he gave up his delinquent life-style.

Coping with Manipulation

Like Danny, children who are able to establish significant relationships to adults, including their child care workers, tend to develop a capacity to control inner urges, thus helping to curb pleasure-seeking patterns of behavior. Before this is achieved, a child will persist in seeking gratifications, even when this attitude may be harmful to himself and others.

Manipulation is a prevalent technique of children in residential settings. For example, if a child finds that his worker does not grant an inappropriate request, he may approach his caseworker, a supervisor or an administrator. How this maneuver is dealt with is important because of the implications for the developing relationship between the child and his child care worker. The child should be told that he has to resolve the issue with his child care worker, or consult him before a decision is made, or ask the worker to review the request. The caseworker then avoids becoming a tool of manipulation and helps the child focus on their relationship. Respect for the child care worker's authority strengthens it and conveys to the child the need to work things through with him directly. This circumscribes the child's operational sphere.

Administrative or supervisory staff may be constructively involved with an individual child for treatment reasons. A child care worker, teacher or therapist may request that a supervisor or administrator see a child to clarify institutional policy against which he may be reacting or which he may question or to reaffirm standards or expectations, or for disciplinary action that requires administrative intervention. Such use of multiple authority roles in residential treatment can be therapeutically advantageous. It is particularly applicable with acting-out, impulsive adolescents, who are generally distrustful of authority (Adler, 1971). The child care worker who is confronted by a child's behavioral difficulties has to decide upon appropriate action related both to the child's treatment needs and the developing relationship between himself and the child. To avoid a threat to the relationship, he may prefer to shift disciplinary responsibility temporarily to his supervisor.

Confronted by a powerful authority figure who may impose limits, including punishment, the child may then turn to his child care worker or to his caseworker, to whom he can express his complaints and hostility against the supervisor. The worker provides the child with an opportunity to discuss the total situation and helps him examine his own role as contributor to the difficulty that resulted in punishment. This places the worker in a more favorable position with the youngster, increasing the child's dependence on him and strengthening their relationship. As the degree of the child's dependence and trust in the worker increases, he is more likely to accept controls from him, eliminating the need for the supervisor's intervention (Adler and Berman, 1960).

When a child care worker requests intervention by a supervisor or administrator because he is fearful or else he does not care to become involved in a situation where firmness and strength on his part have to be exercised, he faces complications. For example, John, the biggest boy in the cottage, refused to do his cottage chores and defied the new worker's efforts (including demands, pleas, and threats) to cooperate. The worker telephoned the cottage supervisor, requesting that he come to the cottage to help him cope with John. When the supervisor entered the cottage, John turned to the worker, disdainfully called him "chicken," and began to work. John's challenge to the worker's authority was purposive, and the latter failed the test. By calling for intervention of a higher authority before fully exploring other possibilities, such as deferment of a head-on confrontation, individual discussion with John, or group involvement in evaluating John's actions, the worker exposed his inexperience as well as his weakness. He left himself open to group resentment and future challenges that might further undermine his authority and therapeutic effectiveness (Adler, 1971).

The interpersonal transactions between an individual child

and his child care worker occur within the context of a group. The adult's actions and reactions are subject to observation and judgment by the other children. If the worker is unfair to a child or openly rejects someone, the others are affected. Even his "favorites" may become uneasy about the permanency of their favored position, and the development of a sense of trust in the worker may be hampered.

Observations of a Child's Relationship Capabilities

1. Does he initiate physical or verbal contact with peers and/or adults? If he does, does he do it appropriately in terms of timing or situation? Is he unreasonable in demanding physical contact, envious of others, over-aggressive, whining?
2. Does he avoid physical contact with peers and adults?
3. Does he ever ask for help from workers? If so, is it appropriate or immature? Is it expressed in a crying or whining tone, and is it generally attention getting?
4. Does he refuse the worker's help?
5. Does he like to help others or does he refuse even when asked?
6. Does he have a "single" friend, many friends or none at all?
7. Does he try to "buy" friendships by giving gifts or acting as a flunky to others?
8. Does he enjoy playing with others or is he a loner?
9. Does he tend to dominate in relationship with others or is he a follower, or the scapegoat of the group?
10. Is he able to compromise in controversial situations? Does he tend to argue uncompromisingly? Or does he withdraw from an argument?
11. Is he cooperative or highly competitive?
12. Is he able to tolerate frustration? If not, does he try

to avoid it? Does he react with anxiety, crying, attack on others or a temper tantrum?

13. Does he adapt to new situations with ease or avoidance?
14. Does he become easily frightened?
15. Is he easily influenced by peers or adults?
16. How does he relate to group pressure?
17. Does he give evidence of a sense of guilt? When it occurs does it seem excessive?
18. Is he capable of learning from experience?
19. Can he control aggressive impulses?
20. Is he capable of expressing affection?
21. Can be tolerate a show of affection toward him?
22. Is he sensitive to other people's feelings?
23. How does he react when he makes a mistake or when he fails at something?
24. How does he react to success?
25. Is he able to admit to wrongdoing?

RELATIONSHIP WITH THE GROUP

Group living is a universal human phenomenon represented in society by social groups ranging in size from families to nations. Residential living is basically group living. The cottage or dormitory group differs from a family group because it is neither biological nor homogeneous. Its members may come from different socioeconomic, cultural, racial or religious backgrounds; its membership is open-ended, with newcomers replacing those who are discharged. Like a family, the group experiences collective living, participates in similar daily routines and responsibilities and joint activities. Since membership is not voluntary but the result of adult selection, effort is required before the group develops a sense of cohesiveness, common interests and identifications.

Dynamics of Group Living

The group is a dynamic entity. Each interaction among the children and between children and staff generates new interactions. The worker must be constantly aware of the dynamic balances and imbalances within his group. A crisis for an individual child has an effect on the group. When a child has to be hospitalized, the rest of the group becomes anxious. When a member of the group is involved in serious delinquency, the group is affected. Continuous evaluation of the group, both as a unit and as a composite of many different individuals who are interacting in a complexity of relationships, is essential.

Adaptation to residential group living presents adjustment problems for all children. It is difficult for the more seriously disturbed; it can be nightmarish for the very deviant or bizarre child. By his very presence the deviant child may pose a threat to the group as a whole or to individual members, because he may arouse latent anxieties that are turned against him in the form of hostile and aggressive acts. Thus the socially immature, physically unattractive girl, placed in a sexually oriented teenage girls' group, evokes annoyance and rejection; the effeminate looking intellectual boy placed in an aggressively oriented boys' group seems to be a threat to the tenuous sense of security of the others. The girl, as well as the boy, is likely to become an object of derision and end up as abused, ridiculed spacegoat.

Every child tends to reenact his conflicts and accustomed patterns of behavior. The delinquent youngster will strive to perpetuate his tendencies within the cottage group by recruiting others to join him in antisocial acts. If a boy with sadistic tendencies is placed in the same room with one who has masochistic traits, it is likely that both will tend to reinforce their pathological needs in their relationship and may even join forces to attack others. An important task here is to estimate whether the relationship between two or more children is based on common disturbances or common strengths. When the latter is the case, the relationship is a wholesome one and should be encouraged. If it is based on common disturbance, the relationship should be discouraged. In some cases, separation into different rooms or even cottage transfer may be required. A cottage group should not be overbalanced with large numbers of children manifesting severe disturbance. It should have a number of children with sufficient ego strengths and positive value orientations to represent a nucleus of wholesome leadership which will enhance and motivate others to follow positive staff and peer values. This is particularly important in pre-adolescent and adolescent groupings. Unless counteracted by adult control, significant relationships and constructive programming, there is a tendency for the informal cottage culture to be dominated by gang leadership, a gang code, and a pecking order of social organization.

Informal Cottage Culture

Adler and Berman (1960, p. 218) describe such an adolescent cottage group:

> There were few constructive goals within the group and energy was dissipated in destructive pursuits and in the maintenance of a delinquent hierarchy against adult authority. Interpersonal relationships in the peer group were strongly authoritarian, with the "strong man" and his lieutenants dominating the group. This clique bullied the weaker youngsters. There was little, if any, respect for the autonomy of the individual. A minimum of democratic processes operated. The group's values were anti-intellectual. Boys who showed a tendency

towards scholastic achievement were ridiculed and those who attempted to move toward more constructive social values faced group disapproval. Thus the group's mores and behavior tended to counteract the therapeutic purposes of the institution.

It is valuable for the child care worker to be aware of the natural leaders, the manipulators, the instigators and scapegoats in their groups, as well as the composition and characteristics of the various subgroups of cliques. One way to increase this understanding is to learn how the children relate to each other in terms of friendship patterns. In the design of such a "sociogram" the children may be asked to rank their cottage peers in terms of role and status. In a cottage of 15, the children could be asked to number a cottage list, with designations from 1-15 of those whom they respect most or least, whom they consider most popular, whom they would like as a roommate or as a playmate during leisure time activities. The children have to be assured that their choices will be confidential and that the staff motive for asking for this information is to facilitate grouping for activities on the basis of preferences. Sociograms could then be charted, giving information regarding status hierarchy in the group. The most favored, the rejects or isolates, the leaders and the scapegoats could then be identified.

Knowledge of the informal cottage culture and the unwritten group "code" is important but not easily achieved. It requires sensitive observation and good relationship with the children. The expectations and practices of the group do not generally conform to the institution's rules and therapeutic objectives. The degree of difference between them may be an index of the effectiveness of the therapeutic program. It may also serve to formulate intervention techniques to help the children modify an anti-therapeutic or destructive code of expectations and behavior.

A key factor in the informal group culture is peer leadership. Constructive leadership should be supported and given encouragement; destructive, delinquent leadership that aims at dominating the group through strong-arm methods should be curbed. If the child care worker is insecure with a youngster in a peer leadership role or, in extreme cases, is afraid of him, he cannot convince the children that he can protect them from leadership abuse. This conviction may not be easy to convey in an older adolescent cottage group because of the potential of physical confrontation. If a worker has misgivings about his capacity to deal with aggressive leadership, he should discuss his feeling with his fellow workers and supervisor. He needs assurance of support and help to understand his anxieties.

Status in the Group

Most children in residential treatment, like their peers in the community who want to be accepted by the status group in school, strive to be accepted by the power group in their cottage. To achieve this, a child may become a "follower" or even a "flunky" of the aggressive in-group which dominates cottage life. According to Mayer (1958, p. 43) the child care worker "has to help each of the followers to recognize that they have a right to be themselves. He has to support them in developing enough security to express their individuality in word and action, even if it differs from expectations of group leaders or adults." He may be able to achieve this by providing opportunities for them to demonstrate leadership qualities, talents or skills which will enhance their status in the group.

The child who is withdrawn or isolated avoids relationship in the group. It takes time and requires patience to help him overcome his misgivings and suspicions. The other children, who may resent the isolate, also need help to understand that his isolation is not due to dislike of them but to his own problems.

The "scapegoat" who evokes hostile attitudes and at times cruel treatment needs protection from attack and abuse from his peers, who will have to be worked with to help them understand that he is being exploited as a result of their own "hang-ups." Group discussion can be helpful in such situations. This was illustrated in a cottage meeting with an adolescent, delinquent-oriented group of boys. The group was talking about their attitude and behavior toward Fred, a weak, physically inadequate effeminate youngster who had recently been admitted to the cottage. At one point, John said: "When someone gets frustrated for some reason, the first thing he does is to seek out a weaker boy to vent his anger on. At the moment, it's Fred who is the target for today." The worker asked whether this was a "mature" way of handling one's angry feelings. There was much more talk about this and at the end of the session, Alan suggested that they continue talking in order to find a better way of coping with their feelings than projecting them at Fred. Fred, like many children who achieve the scapegoat status in a group may actually be unconsciously provoking antagonistic attitudes and even physical attack. This requires intervention by both child care workers and therapists.

Group Meetings

Verbal exchange should be encouraged with opportunities for discussion regarding strains and frustrations of group living. Regularly scheduled cottage meetings are valuable. These generally focus on issues related to cottage living. Topics for discussion include planning programs, evaluating cottage work assignments, crisis situations, preparing for new arrivals or departures, making decisions related to the cottage, examining common concerns such as violations of rules and routines, scapegoating, sex play, bizarre behavior on the part of individual children or subgroups.

The following is a report of interactions in a cottage group meeting with an aggressive group of boys:

> We were talking about Sid, who was being mistreated by a number of the boys. Jim said that they didn't like Sid because he was "crazy." For example, the other day he had said to them, "Go ahead, hurt me until I break down and am sent to the hospital." The worker asked, "Isn't it sad that Sid had to say he'd rather be hurt so much that he would have to be sent to a hospital than remain in the cottage taking abuse from some of you!" After a minute's silence Phil burst out with "It's tragic! Why can't you guys treat him better? He doesn't try to hurt anyone." Paul jumped up from his seat and he said, "I know what the trouble is. We are just a bunch of delinquents. We are not used to boys like this one. We come from different families than he so we don't like him. He seems helpless and we pick on him and we hurt him." Barry muttered under his breath that he was "ashamed of this bunch, ashamed of being in the cottage." The worker turned to Barry and said "Barry, what did you say? Say it out loud." He got up and told the boys what he felt. He accused them of misunderstanding Sid, who couldn't help being different. What they were doing to him wasn't fair.

Acording to Fant (1971, p. 78), a basic requirement in group meetings is that "freedom of expression must be encouraged, with cottage staff interceding only at those points where they feel that the excitement and stimulation emanating from the discussion will cause the group to suffer from overhelming guilt, anxiety, fear or despair." This does not imply passivity on the part of the adult participants. An active role is frequently required to overcome resistances to communication among a disturbed group of children.

Another type of group meeting which Fant calls "small, spontaneous interview group" involves subgroups in the cottage convened to discuss destructive acting out. "These groups, or more appropriately, cliques, bring out various behavior patterns directed at themselves, their worker, another child or another subgroup. The worker in the cottage, whenever possible, should isolate the subgroup and non-punitively highlight their behavior, helping them see the implications of what they have been doing or how they are using each other in the group" (Fant, 1971, p. 79).

This type of meeting applies Fritz Redl's life-space interview concept to a group (Redl, 1966, pp. 35-67). The life-space interview deals with crisis situations and is built around a child's direct life experience in connection with a crisis issue, which then becomes the interview focus. It is most effective when conducted by a person who is "perceived by the child as part of his natural habitat of life-space, and with some pretty clear role and power in his daily living, as contrasted to the therapist, to whom he is sent for long-range treatment" (Redl, 1966, p. 41). The child care worker is such a person. In a crisis situation, his immediate availability can be therapeutic. It represents support to a child at a time of severe emotional stress; it may offer understanding at a point of greatest receptivity. On the other hand, postponing therapeutic intervention to the child's next scheduled therapy session may represent a loss. By that time the child's perception of the incident may be blurred or distorted, the generated conflict may be repressed, and the experienced emotions denied. The child care worker's interaction with the child does not exclude further follow-up of the incident in therapy sessions.

Privacy

One of the problems of residential living is lack of privacy. It is important for a child to be by himself, to be able to think, read, work or play in privacy. This is difficult in group living because of physical limitations of space or requirements regarding accountability. The latter refers to programs where the child care workers are held responsible for knowing at all times the whereabouts of every child. Accountability is important for safety, and when interpreted as such conveys to children adult concern and caring. But when it is used as a rationale for adult control, or when it is based on suspicion and lack of confidence in children's capabilities to be alone without getting into mischief, it is neither helpful nor therapeutic. In fact, it feeds childhood distrust. As much as possible, opportunities should be provided for a child to be by himself in his own room, or in a corner in a common room, or outside the cottage. Occasional informal checks by the workers should meet accountability requirements. A period of each day should be scheduled as "free time" to allow children to pursue individual activity of interest to them.

Ethnic and Religious Differences

Cultural, ethnic and religious diversity are also important in group living. Each child's heritage and identity deserve respect and attention. When the population of an institution is heterogeneous, as most are today, the total program should take into consideration the varied identities among the children. The religious education program provides classes and services for each major religious group. Religious holidays are given recognition so that each religious group can celebrate according to its customs. Food should reflect cultural diversity, not only to meet the tastes of a particular group but also to acquaint the other children with a variety of foods. Above all, staff attitudes should reflect tolerance and respect for all differences. The benefits derived go beyond a responsibility to provide reinforcement of the children's cultural, ethnic and religious identities. They reflect pluralism in democratic living. The entire population is enriched by education in diversity, and the practice of tolerance.

Cultural diversity can also have a direct impact on cottage living. To quote Steinfeld (1975):

> More than any other factor, the quality of institutional life and group care is determined by the way the children treat one another. Therefore, the major task of all staff is enabling children to live together in peace. This requires acceptable outlets for aggression and frustration, opportunities for learning, growth and achievement of self-esteem. All this leads to an acceptance of difference or the assurance that the unique or even provocative aspects of an individual are no personal threat, but in fact a source of fascination. The behavior, race, language, religion, home background of one's roommate or classmate, however different, are not fearful. I have found that the religious and cultural diversity of children offers a special opportunity to communicate these concepts of respect for difference, and so transform fear and hatred of one's peers to creative group living.

Oversensitivity, insecurity and uncertainty about dealing with ethnic differences may at times immobilize a child care worker. Burns (1971, p. 93) states: "There is no magic that can prevent confusion, conflict and anxiety around racial situations at this time. However, there are some points to be made: All workers, no matter what their classification, need constantly to look at and try to face their true attitudes and biases. Black workers as well as white workers have problems in working with black children." Burns recounts an experience with one of his workers, who was white, who had difficulty in handling a small group of black children. He was not setting required limits because he was worried that he would be judged unfair by black children and black staff. Burns told him, "Forget that these children are black and treat them as you would treat other children who have similar problems." To treat these children differently, Burns felt, was to be overly permissive and to "practice discrimination in reverse" (Burns, 1971, p. 92).

In summary, the group is the focus of the child care worker's tasks; the welfare of the individual child is his primary concern. According to Lemay (1974, p. 37), "The group, while being the unit of work, is not an end in itself. It is a *therapeutic tool*." The group becomes the medium for each child's growth and development. This is achievable only when through the efforts of the child care workers the cottage milieu emanates an atmosphere of acceptance, warmth and sensitivity to the children's needs as individuals and as a group, provides a sense of security for all the children, and encourages child participation in issues of group living.

RELATIONS WITH PARENTS

A child's emotional difficulties cannot be viewed apart from his family. To understand the children we treat, we must understand their families. To treat the children effectively, we must work with their families. Even the physically handicapped and mentally retarded children who are in residence primarily as a consequence of their individual handicaps have been affected by family reactions to them as handicapped children. In these cases, there has either been overprotection or neglect and rejection, or a combination of all of these, which the children will reflect in terms of their self-concept and attitude toward others.

Parental Reaction to Placement

Parental problems account for most placements of children in foster care. This is particularly true of children designated as dependent or neglected who are in placement in foster homes, group homes, group residences, and general institutions. On the other hand, the major reasons for placement in institutions for the mentally retarded, or in residential treatment centers for emotionally disturbed children, are considered to be within the children themselves (Bernstein et al., 1975, p. 11). A clear dichotomy cannot be made between a child's and his parent's problems because both interrelate and contribute to the circumstances which may eventually lead to a decision to place the child in placement.

Understanding of a child's background, including family experience, school and neighborhood relationships, is helpful to the child care worker. This information should be available to him through the child's caseworker. It is particularly important because by his role he approximates a parental figure; further, many of the children in residential treatment project distorted images of parenthood upon their child care workers. If, through his expressed attitudes and behavior, a child care worker resembles the child's actual parent, with whom he was in conflict, it is more likely that the child will try to replicate his accustomed destructive relationship patterns in his relationship with the worker.

Residential treatment involves sensitive and complex relationships with parents. The way parents feel about placing their child has important implications for the course of his adjustment. Parents who were unable to manage a child may feel guilty about their failure. They handle this guilt in a variety of ways. Some try to alleviate it by viewing the residence as the "perfect" place, so that they will feel better about placing their child. Such parents are pleasant to child care workers.

Others will make up for their guilt feelings by overindulging their children during visits, helping them violate regulations, giving them extra money, and collaborating with them in their attempt to perpetuate pathological patterns of behavior. Still others must maintain the delusion that their child alone is responsible for his failings and that no one can succeed with him. They tend to look for difficulties in the child's adjustment in the institution and negate his progress in order to convince themselves that he cannot be helped by anyone. They disparage the institution and its staff to the child; in this way they attempt to sabotage his efforts to adapt and to benefit from treatment. Such parents seem to have a stake in perpetuating their child's emotional disturbance.

Many parents whose children were committed through the courts against their wishes may not be cooperative. The most difficult are those who will complain to administration about residential staff, send complaints to the city and state agencies, and collect grievances in order to prove that their child should not be in placement. Such parents make treatment for their children most difficult. It is advisable for child care staff to keep a polite and reserved distance from them. They are masters at provoking antagonistic feelings. When these are expressed, they complain of being mistreated. Personal reactions should be discussed with one's supervisor and the child's caseworker, and *not* be displaced onto their children. A child care worker, irritated constantly by such parents, may understandably wish they would take their child home. While this would remove a taxing experience for staff, it would be harmful to the child.

Home Visits

Families are involved through casework with parents, home visits by the children and visiting by parents. Home visits provide an opportunity for children to be with their parents for weekends or during holidays. These family reunions are discussed and the interactions examined in casework sessions with parents and children separately, and, when feasible, in family treatment sessions including the child, his parents and siblings. Home visits can also be used by the child to evaluate changes in attitudes toward parents and former friends in the neighborhood. They should be planned carefully according to the child's needs and the family's capacity to cope with his presence. Regularly scheduled visits take place where warranted. It is important that the child's caseworker be aware of the way the child makes use of the home visits and how he and his family spend time at home. Misuse of home visits by children, or neglect or abuse of children during home visits should be discussed with the child and his parents; a decision is then made as to whether the home visits should be suspended, reduced or eliminated.

Parent Visiting

In most settings, visiting by parents generally takes place on weekends when the professional staff does not work. In certain institutions a caseworker is on duty during parent visiting time to permit discussions of their children's adjustment and progress. The degree of interaction between child care workers and parents depends on the established policies of a particular setting. A friendly relationship is encouraged in most places. The worker has to be selective about the information he conveys to the visitors because he cannot know whether a parent will use it destructively or distort what was said, or how the child will view an exchange of information about him.

Observation by the worker of the interaction between a child and his parents is important and should be recorded or reported to caseworkers. The following are suggested guidelines.

1. How does the child relate to his visitors? Is he actively hostile, distant, indifferent, or is he happy to see them?

The same observation should apply to attitude and behavior of the parents or siblings toward the child.

2. What is the effect of the visit on the child? Is he anxious before the visitors arrive? Is he distressed, angry or happy after the parental visit?

3. Observation regarding a child's reactions before or after home visits is also important. If he is anxious before the visit or distressed after he returns to the institution, this should be reported to the caseworker for further follow-up.

RELATIONSHIPS WITH STAFF OF OTHER DISCIPLINES

Interdisciplinary communication is important in residential treatment. The child care worker not only consults with social workers, teachers and recreational workers but also has contact with nurses, psychiatrists, psychologists, supervisory and administrative personnel, housekeeping, clerical and maintenance staff, and the director. The following is a general description of the role and function of staff with whom the child care worker may interact. Functions may vary in different settings.

Caseworkers

The caseworker is involved with children from intake through discharge and frequently in aftercare services. He sees the child regularly and is this therapist in many settings; he is in contact with the child's family and, if necessary, community agencies; he is responsible for maintaining the child's case record, for writing reports to cooperating agencies, and for the preparation of required statistical reporting for administrative and research purposes.

Cooperation and continuous interchange of information between child care workers and caseworkers are of utmost importance in the realization of established treatment goals. The caseworker's knowledge of the child's history, his family and his feelings and attitudes and the child care worker's observations of the child's functioning should be freely shared. Child care information of interest to caseworkers includes the following:

1. Problems related to physical care such as grooming and overall personal hygiene.
2. Sleep routines, including problems regarding falling asleep or waking.
3. Food idiosyncracies, including food fads, overeating or undereating, and behavior while dining.
4. Use of leisure time, including the child's interests, and his attitude in recreational and play activities.
5. Adaptability to cottage routines.
6. Relationship with cottage staff, viz. his attitude toward them: does he cling or withdraw, is he hostile or does he comply passively? Does he tend to manipulate or to be cooperative?
7. Relationship with peers, including his capacity for friendship, leadership role and acceptability by others.
8. Reactions during parental visits.
9. Reaction to illness and prescribed medication.

Teachers

Generally, children in residential treatment settings have experienced frustration and partial or complete failure in community schools. Consequently, they come to view education with reservations. They have misgivings about their learning capacities and preconceived stereotypes about teachers. There is apt to be little contact between child care workers and teachers if the children attend off-ground school. Where education takes place within the institution, communication between them is facilitated. Interchange of information with teachers and involvement in the child's education process convey to children that their child care workers are interested in their learning.

Medical

Child care workers are involved with the medical services through scheduled sick-call at the infirmary, emergencies, preventive medicine, and accidents. They are generally first to become aware of a child's complaints about not feeling well; they bring him to the infirmary for examination and treatment; they may dispense medication.

Psychiatrists

The psychiatrist usually functions as a consultant to staff. He sees individual children for diagnostic purposes, or, in crisis situations, prescribes medication, and when necessary arranges for psychiatric hospitalization. As a member of the residential treatment team he participates in treatment planning and evaluation conferences. He is also involved in staff training and may carry some treatment cases.

Psychologists

Psychologists are responsible for psychological testing for psychodiagnostic purposes and may also function as therapists and consultants.

Recreation Workers

The number and type of recreation specialists depend on the size and scope of the institution's program. When recreation is provided by a separate department, child care workers may be involved in consulting recreation staff regarding their children's functioning. They are responsible for supervising children's movements to scheduled activities and for orienting activity group leaders to an individual child's needs, attitudes and behavior in group situations. In turn, recreation leaders should inform child care workers of a child's functioning in activities, development of skills, relationship to other children, and anxieties evoked by certain activities. They can also be helpful as resource persons in planning leisure time cottage activities.

Religious Workers

The religious program, comprising religious education and services, provides opportunities for continuity of children's religious identification. Child care workers accompany children to religious services. Consultation with the religious workers regarding children's religious attitudes can be helpful.

Other Personnel

The child care worker also has occasion to deal with institutional personnel not directly involved in the treatment of children, such as housekeepers, dining room and kitchen staff, office and maintenance workers.

Interdisciplinary Conferences

Periodic interdisciplinary conferences on individual children are most important occasions for staff consultation. The child care worker, like the other members of the team, presents a concise and comprehensive report regarding a child's functioning within his area of responsibility. He discusses the child's cottage relationships, symptomatic behavior, attitudes toward work, overall behavior, parental visiting. He has the opportunity to seek clarification on questions and to ask for guidelines on helping the child in situations which may be troublesome.

Child care workers have at times complained that too much conference time is devoted to review of a child's history, diagnosis and psychodynamics, leaving little time for discussing methods of dealing with the difficult behavior. The child care worker should not hesitate to ask for discussion and guidance to help him deal with disturbances which are disruptive and distressing to staff and children. Specific solutions are not always possible, but if such discussion takes place, the child care worker may feel that he is not isolated or unsupported. Any suggestions that are made will represent collective concern and responsibility which are the true measure of "integration."

Child Care Supervisor

The child care supervisor is responsible for the professional development, supervision and evaluation of his child care staff. He orients the child care worker to child care tasks and the philosophy and practices of residential treatment. He helps him develop the knowledge, skills and attitudes appropriate to his functions, to organize his work for optimum effectiveness and to derive satisfaction from a job well done. He may also act as the child care worker's advocate with administration and as his link to other members of the residential treatment team.

The quality of the relationship between a child care worker and his supervisor is a crucial determinant of its benefit to him as well as the children. A sense of trust is essential for openness in communicating, for frankness in expressing feelings, and for confidence that one will be listened to with sympathy. In such an atmosphere, situations can be discussed objectively, errors examined without fear and with a sense of comfort that one can learn from mistakes.

The following is a suggested outline for supervisory discussions of child-worker interaction. It may be used to evaluate situations with a group as well as with individual children.

FACTUAL DESCRIPTION

1. Describe the incident.
2. What action did you take?
3. What was the outcome? On the child, on the group (if other children were involved or witnessed the incident)?

Analysis of the Incident

1. What do you think made the child act as he did? (What is your interpretation of his behavior—its motive and objective?)
2. What was your feeling toward the child at the time of the incident?
3. What were the reasons for the action you took? (What did you try to achieve?)
4. Were there alternative actions you could have taken?
5. How did you feel after it was over?
6. How did the child act toward you after the incident?
7. If other children observed the situation, how did they react to the child and to you?
8. If another worker was on duty with you and observed the incident, what was his reaction?
9. If the incident was a crisis situation or had consequences which were distressing, do you now think it could have been foreseen and the crisis prevented? How?

Generally, child care workers meet with their supervisors for regularly scheduled individual and/or group conferences, and as needed for special and emergency situations. Evaluation conferences are also held periodically to assess work performance. According to Mayer (1958, pp. 160-61), these should cover a wide range of subjects, including the worker's relationship with individual children, the group and his co-workers, his management and organizational capabilities in the cottage, and his ability to function within the administrative structure of the agency. They should convey to the worker his strengths and the progress he has made, as well as weaknesses and areas requiring improvement.

REFERENCES

ADLER, JACK, "Separation—A Crucial Issue in Foster Care." *Journal of Jewish Communal Service*, Vol. 46, No. 4, 1970, pp. 305-313.

ADLER, JACK, "Interpersonal Relationships in Residential Treatment Centers for Disturbed Children." *Child Welfare*, Vol. 50, No. 4, 1971, pp. 208-217.

ADLER, JACK, and BERMAN, IRWIN, "Ego-Superego Dynamics in Residential Treatment of Disturbed Adolescents." (mimeographed). Presented at the 37th Annual Meeting of American Orthopsychiatric Assn., 1960.

ADLER, JACK, and BERMAN, IRWIN, "Multiple Leadership in Group Treatment of Delinquent Adolescents." *The International Journal of Group Psychotherapy*, Vol. 19, No. 2, pp. 213-226.

BERNSTEIN, BLANCHE, SNIDER, DONALD A., and MEEZAN, WILLIAM, *A Preliminary Report—Foster Care Needs and Alternatives to Placement*, N.Y. State Board of Social Welfare, June, 1975.

BRENDTRO, LARRY K., "Establishing Relationship Beachheads." In *The Other 23 Hours*, Treischman, Albert E., Whittaker, James K. and Brendtro, Larry K., editors, Chicago, Aldine, 1969.

BURNS, CRAWFORD E., "White Staff, Black Children; Is There a Problem?" *Child Welfare*, Vol. 50, No. 2, 1971, pp. 90-96.

FANT, RAYMOND, S., "Use of Groups in Residential Treatment." In *Healing Through Living*, Mayer, M.F. and Blum, A., editors, Springfield, Ill. Charles C Thomas, 1971, pp. 72-93.

LEMAY, MICHAEL, *The Functions of the Specialized "Educateur" for Maladjusted Youth*. English translation by Vivian Jarvis, Green Chimneys School, Brewster, N.Y., November 1974, (mimeographed).

LITTNER, N., *Traumatic Effects of Separation and Placement*. New York, Child Welfare League of America, 1950.

MAHLER, MARGARET S. and LA PERRIERE, K., "Mother-Child Interaction during Separation-Individuation." *Psychoanalytic Quarterly*, Vol. 34, 1965, pp. 483-497.

MANDELBAUM, ARTHUR, "Parent Child Separation: Its Significance to Parents." *Social Work*, Vol. 7, No. 4, 1962, pp. 27-34.

MAYER, MORRIS, F., *A Guide for Child Care Workers*. New York, Child Welfare League of America, 1958.

REDL, FRITZ, *When We Deal with Children*. New York, The Free Press, 1966.

STEINFELD, PAUL, "Relevance of Residential Treatment." Unpublished paper presented at the National Conference of Jewish) Communal Service, Grossinger's, N.Y. June 10, 1975 (mimeographed).

Appendix: Diagnostic Classification

Diagnosis of Mental Disorders

In residential treatment, child care workers become familiar with diagnosis through consultation with social workers, psychologists and psychiatrists, participation in conferences and reading of case records. The following diagnostic classification is based on the official nomenclature of the American Psychiatric Association (1968).

The description of the major categories of mental disorders is followed by those specifically applicable to children and adolescents.

I. *Psychoses*

A psychosis represents severe impairment in mental functioning which grossly interferes with adaptation and adjustment to demands of daily living. What is crucial is the severity of impairment of the major ego functions in relation to reality, thinking processes, control of instinctual drives, interpersonal relationships and the synthetic function by which the ego mediates between the demands of instinctual drives (the id), internalized parental and social prohibitions (the superego or conscience) and the demands of external reality. (The ego represents mental mechanisms which have to do with the individual's relation to the environment.) There is an impairment in awareness or ability to cope with reality in self-care, work and relationships. The presence of thinking disorders like hallucinations and delusions distorts perceptions. Severe mood swings interfere with responses to oneself and to others. There may also be impairment in thinking, language and memory.

Psychoses are classified in two broad categories—those associated with organic brain symptoms and the so-called functional psychoses which are not attributed to physical conditions. The major category, schizophrenia, occurs in childhood and adolescence.

Schizophrenia: Schizophrenia is characterized by severe impairment of the ego functions, and is subdivided into a number of types. Among them are: simple, hebephrenic, catatonic, paranoid and childhood. In schizophrenia, childhood type, schizophrenic symptoms appear before puberty. A child suffering from this condition manifests unevenness and gross immaturity in development. There may also be atypical, bizarre and withdrawn behavior.

Another condition not designated in the American Psychiatric Association Manual, but frequently referred to in relation to severe childhood disorders, is "borderline state" or "borderline schizophrenia." This describes a condition similar to schizophrenia but different from it in scope, severity and constancy of ego function impairment. Scope means that not all the ego functions are impaired; constancy connotes less regularity in the impairment of the ego functions than in schizophrenia (Silverman et al., pp. 7-8).

II. *Personality Disorders*

This group of mental disorders is characterized by deeply ingrained maladaptive patterns or character traits. These are generally lifelong patterns in evidence by the time of preadolescence. In contrast to psychosis, reality function is not impaired.

The major categories of personality disorders are:

1. *Antisocial Personality*—behavior is antisocial, involves the person in conflict with society; there is uncontrolled impulsivity, a tendency to blame others for his own misdeeds and a lack of capacity for loyalty to others and to social values.

2. *Passive Aggressive Personality*—passivity and aggressiveness characterize the overall behavior. Aggressiveness is generally expressed passively through avoidance, obstructionism and inattention.

3. *Hysterical Personality*—characterized by self-centeredness, immaturity, excitability, overdependence.

4. *Obsessive-Compulsive Personality*—characterized by excessive concern with conformity, rigidity, extreme conscientiousness and inability to relax.

5. *Schizoid Personality*—shyness, seclusiveness, oversensitivity, avoidance of close relationships, inability to express aggressive feelings and hostility.

6. *Paranoid Personality*—rigid, unwarranted suspicion, excessive envy, projection of blame on others.

7. *Explosive Personality*—excitable, aggressive, prone to outbursts of rage and physical and verbal aggression.

III. *Neuroses*

The neuroses do not involve severe impairment in ego functions. Anxiety is the chief characteristic. It may be felt and expressed directly or defended against by unconsciously controlled mechanisms called "defense mechanisms." These produce symptoms experienced as distress. The major defense mechanisms include:

1. *Denial*—exclusion from consciousness of a feeling, thought, wish, need or external reality which is consciously intolerable.

2. *Displacement*—an emotion is transferred from its original object to a more acceptable substitute. For example, if a child is angry with a parent, he'll strike another child because it is safer to do so.

3. *Projection*—the individual attributes a personal wish or impulse to some other person or object because it is emotionally unacceptable to the self.

4. *Repression*—unacceptable ideas or wishes, memories, feelings or impulses are barred from consciousness. Repressed

material may emerge in disguised form. It reduces the effectiveness of the ego because it requires expenditures of psychic energy to keep the repressed from entering consciousness.

5. *Intellectualization*—reasoning is used as a defense against the confrontation with an unconscious conflict. There is overemphasis on ideational content, often unrelated to the impulse.

6. *Rationalization*—a tendency to explain away impulses. A particular act or thought is attributed to a motive different from the one which is actually responsible for the act.

7. *Isolation*—an unacceptable impulse, idea, thought or act is separated from its original memory source, removing the emotion associated with the original memory from consciousness.

8. *Regression*—a partial symbolic return to more infantile patterns of reacting.

9. *Compensation*—the individual attempts to make up for real or fancied deficiencies.

10. *Undoing*—an attempt to disprove or undo harm which the individual unconsciously imagines or consciously perceives. It may be expressed in ritualistic behavior.

11. *Sublimation*—instinctual drives unconsciously unacceptable are diverted into personally satisfying, socially acceptable, channels of expression.

Although persons suffering from neuroses may be severely handicapped by symptoms, they (unlike the psychotic) are aware that they are mentally disturbed and want to be relieved of experiencing the anxiety caused by the symptoms.

The following are major types of neuroses:

1. *Phobic Neurosis*—intense fear of an object or situation is characteristic of this condition. Despite the fact that the person consciously knows that there is no real danger when confronted by the phobic object situation (animal, heights, crowds, school in the case of children), he experiences

severe anxiety in the form of nausea, faintness, palpitation and panic. The phobic object or situation represents a displacement from an object or situation of which the person is unaware.

2. *Obsessive Compulsive Neurosis*—A person suffering from obsessive compulsive neurosis is unable to keep out of his consciousness the intrusion of an unacceptable thought, urge or action. The action is driven by an uncontrollable urge varying from simple acts to complex rituals like hand washing, compulsive cleaning, etc. If a person is prevented from completing his compulsive ritual, he experiences extreme anxiety.

3. *Hysterical Neurosis*—alterations may occur in the patient's state of consciousness or in his sense of identity. Symptoms such as amnesia, sleepwalking, fugue states and multiple personality may be manifested.

4. *Hypochondriacal Neurosis*—there is preocupation with the body and the fear of presumed diseases.

IV. *Transient Situational Disturbances*

These disturbances range in severity, occur in individuals without any apparent underlying mental disorders and represent an acute reaction to overwhelming environmental stress. The symptoms recede after the stressful situation is over. These disorders are classified on the basis of the different stages of personality development.

1. *Adjustment Reaction of Infancy* may be a brief reaction associated with separation from the mother expressed by crying spells, loss of appetite and severe withdrawal.

2. *Adjustment Reaction of Childhood* may be expressed by enuresis, fear of being left alone or abandoned, clinging, to mother, and extreme attention-getting behavior. It may be precipitated by separation, birth of a sibling, etc.

3. *Adjustment Reaction of Adolescence*—Manifestations such as irritability, depression, brooding, loss of confidence,

temper outbursts may follow a traumatic experience such as a breakup with a boyfriend or girlfriend, school failure, death of a significant person.

V. Behavior Disorders of Childhood and Adolescence

These disorders are characterized by a range of symptoms, including overactivity, shyness, inattentiveness, feelings of rejection, aggressiveness, timidity, and delinquency. The major types of this disorder are:

1. *Hyperkinetic Reaction of Childhood or Adolescence* is characterized by overactivity, restlessness, distractability, and short attention span. It is more prevalent in young children than in adolescents.

2. *Withdrawing Reaction of Childhood or Adolescence* includes seclusiveness, detachment, sensitivity, shyness, timidity and general inability to form close relationships.

3. *Overanxious Reaction of Childhood or Adolescence* is characterized by chronic anxiety, excessive unrealistic fears, sleeplessness, and nightmares. There is a lack of self-confidence, inhibitions, apprehensiveness of new situations and unfamiliar surroundings.

4. *Runaway Reaction of Childhood or Adolescence*—Running away from home seems to be the characteristic way to avoid or escape from a threatening situation. These children feel rejected, friendless and inadequate.

5. *Unsocialized Aggressive Reaction of Childhood or Adolescence*—Hostility, disobedience, aggressiveness, destructiveness, stealing, lying, teasing or hurting other children are some of the common characteristics.

6. *Group Delinquent Reaction of Childhood or Adolescence* involves identification and association with a delinquent peer group or gang to whom children are loyal. There is stealing, truancy, vandalism, staying out late at night, and, among girls, promiscuity.

VI. *Mental Retardation*

When classified in accordance with the range of intelligence, it is categorized as follows:

> borderline mental retardation—IQ 68-83
> mild mental retardation—IQ 52-67
> moderate mental retardation—IQ 36-51
> severe mental retardation—IQ 20-35
> profound mental retardation—IQ under 20

Characterization by IQ alone is insufficient in making a diagnosis of mental retardation. The child's developmental history, current adaptive behavior, emotional reactions, verbal and motor skills, and family, school and social relationships must be taken into consideration.

REFERENCES

American Psychiatric Association, *Diagnostic and Statistical Manual of Mental Disorders*, 2nd Edition, Washington, D.C., 1968.

SILVERMAN, LLOYD, LANDER, JOSEPH, ADLER, JACK, ROSMARIN, SAMUEL, BERMAN, IRWIN, GREENSPON, WILLIAM, GOODMAN, MELVIN, CHERBULIEZ, THEODORE, *Diagnostic Manual for the Hawthorne Cedar Knolls School*, 1962 (mimeographed).

Recommended
Bibliography

ADLER, JACK, "Interpersonal Relationships in Residential Treatment Centers." *Child Welfare,* Vol. 50, No. 4, pp. 208-217, 1970.

ADLER, JACK, "Separation, Crucial Issues in Foster Care." *Journal of Jewish Communal Services,* Vol. 46, No. 4, pp. 305-313, 1970.

ADLER, JACK, "The Child Care Counselor as Target of Transferred Behavior." *Child Care Quarterly,* Vol. 2, No. 2, pp. 98-102, 1973.

ALT, HERSCHEL, *Residential Treatment for the Disturbed Child.* New York, International Universities Press, 1960.

AICHORN, AUGUST, *Wayward Youth. New York,* Viking Press, 1934.

ALLERHAND, MELVINE, WEBER, RUTH, & HAUG, MARIE, *Adaptation and Adaptability.* New York: Child Welfare League of America, 1966.

American Association for Children's Residential Centers, *From Chaos to Order: A Collective View of the Residential Treatment of Children.* New York: Child Welfare League of America, 1972.

BEKER, JFROME, GITLESON, PAUL M., KAMINSTEIN, PAUL and
FINKEL ADLER, LOIS, *Critical Incidents in Child Care, A Case
Book.* New York, Behavioral Publications, 1972.

BETTELHEIM, BRUNO, *Love is Not Enough.* Glencoe, Ill., Free
Press, 1950.

BETTELHEIM, BRUNO, *Truants from Life.* Glencoe, Ill., Free Press,
1955.

BETTELHEIM, BRUNO, *A Home for the Heart.* New York, Knopf,
1974.

BILLINGSLEY, ANDREW, *Black Families in White America.* Englewood Cliffs, N.J., Prentice Hall, 1968.

BIRNBACH, DAVID, "The Skill of Child Care." *In The Practice of
Group Work.* Schwartz, William and Zalba, Serapio, R. New
York, (Eds.) Columbia University Press, 1971.

BURMEISTER, EVA, *Tough Times and Tender Moments in Child
Care.* New York, Columbia University Press, 1967.

BURMEISTER, EVA, *The Professional House Parent.* New York,
Columbia University Press, 1960.

BURNS, CRAWFORD E., "White Staff, Black Children; Is There a
Problem?" *Child Welfare,* Vol. 50, No. 2, pp. 90-96, 1971.

D'AMATO, GABRIEL, *Residential Treatment for Child Mental
Health.* Springfield, Ill., Charles C Thomas, 1969.

DINNAGE, ROSEMARIE and PRINGLE, M. L. KELLMER, *Residential
Child Care: Facts and Fallacies.* London, Longmans, 1967.

ERIKSON, ERIK H. *Childhood and Society.* New York, W. W.
Norton, 1963.

FOSTER, GENEVIEVE W., VANDERVEN, KAREN, DAHLBERG,
KRONER, ELEANOR R., CARBONARA, NANCY T. and COHEN,
GEORGE M., *Child Care Work with Emotionally Disturbed
Children.* Pittsburgh, University of Pittsburg Press, 1972.

GOLDFARB, WILLIAM, MINTZ IRVING and STROOCK, CATHERINE
W., *A Time to Heal; Corrective Socialization; A Treatment
Approach to Childhood Schizophrenia.* New York, Interna-
tional Universities Press, 1969.

HYLTON, LYDIA F., *The Residential Treatment Center.* New York
Child Welfare League of America, 1964.

LINTON, THOMAS E., "The European Educateur Program for Disturbed Children." *American Journal of Orthopsychiatry*, Vol. 39, No. 1, pp. 125-33, 1969.

MAYER, MORRIS F., *A Guide for Child Care Workers*, New York, Child Welfare League of America, 1958.

MAYER, MORRIS F. and BLUM, ARTHUR, (Eds.) *Healing Through Living*. Springfield, Ill., Charles C Thomas, 1971.

MINUCHIN, SALVADOR, MONTALVO, BRAULIO, GUERNEY, BERNARD G. JR., ROSMAN, BERNICE and SCHUMER, FLORENCE, *Families of the Slums*, New York, Basic Books, 1967.

POLSKY, HOWARD, *Cottage Six: The Social System of Delinquent Boys in Residential Treatment*. New York, Russell Sage Foundation, 1962.

POLSKY, HOWARD and CLASTER, DANIEL, *The Dynamics of Residential Treatment: A Social System Analysis*. Chapel Hill, University of North Carolina Press, 1968.

REDL, FRITZ and WINEMAN, DAVID, *The Aggressive Child*. Glencoe, Ill., Free Press, 1967.

TOIGO, A., "The Dynamics of the Residential Institution: A System Theory Approach." *Child Care Quarterly*, Vol. 1, No. 3, pp. 252-263, 1972.

TREISCHMAN, ALBERT E. and WHITTAKER, JAMES, K. *Children Away from Home. Chicago*, Aldine Press, 1972.

TREISCHMAN, ALBERT E., WHITTAKER, JAMES K., and BRENDTRO, LARRY K., *The Other 23 Hours*. Chicago, Aldine Press, 1969.

Index

191

Medical staff, 173
Medication, 135-138
 side effects, 137-138
Mellaril, 136, 137
Mental retardation, 185
Mildly retarded, 60
Money, spending, 69-70
Morphine, 141

Neuroses, 181-182
Newcomer to cottage, 149

Parents, 167-171
 reaction to placement, 168
 visiting, 170
Peer leadership, 161
Personal hygiene, 68
Personality disorders, 180-181
Phenothiazines, 136
Play, 71
Poverty, 24
Power struggle, 86
Problem behavior, 98-116
 bedwetting, 104-105
 lying, 107-108
 running away, 111-117
 soiling, 105
 stealing, 109-111
 temper tantrum, 99-103
Privacy, 165
Profane language, 121-122
Projection, 151
Psychiatrist, 173
Psycho-educateur, 12-13
Psychologists, 173
Psychotherapeutic services, 1
Psychoses, 179-180
Puberty, 18
Punishment, 86-95
 criteria, 88
 definition, 85
 group, 89-90
 physical, 90-95
 preventive intervention, 87

Rationalization, 182
Reality, 21
Recording, 198-201

Recreation, 71-81
 co-ed activities, 129-130
 in-cottage, 73-76
 program, 72-73
 workers, 173
Regression, 181
Repression, 181
Relatedness, 21
Relationships, 147-178
 caseworkers, 171
 definition, 151
 individual child, 150-157
 group, 157-167
 parents, 167-171
 staff, 171
 teachers, 172
Residential team, 11
Residential treatment, 12
 concepts, 2-13
Retarded, mildly, 28-29
Runaways, 111-115
 prevention, 112
 reasons for, 112-113

Scapegoat, 162
Scheduled day, 46-47
Schizophrenia, 179
 borderline, 179
 childhood, 27, 179
Sedatives, 136
Self awareness, 41
Separation, 147-149
 children's reactions, 147-148
 orienting newcomers, 149
 parental feelings, 149
Sex education program, 130-132
Sexual behavior, 117
 and aggression, 119-120
 heterosexuality, 127-130
 homosexuality, 123-127
 masturbation, 119
Socialization, corrective, 27
Soiling, 105-106
Spending money, 69-70
Sports, 75
Stealing, 109-111
Stelazine, 136-137
Street-wise child, 4
Structure, 11-13